T0113693

REVERSE MISSION:

THE
DIALECTICS
OF THE
NIGERIAN
RELIGIOSCAPE

NELSON OLUSEGUN
ADEWOLE

authorHOUSE®

AuthorHouse™
1663 Liberty Drive
Bloomington, IN 47403
www.authorhouse.com
Phone: 833-262-8899

Published by AuthorHouse 08/05/2022

ISBN: 978-1-6655-6737-4 (sc)
ISBN: 978-1-6655-6738-1 (e)

ENDORSEMENT

It is obvious that Pentecostalism according to this work is a force to reckon with in the contemporary Christianity. No doubt it has created permanent positive and negative impact on the mainline churches therefore; religious landscape cannot be the same again. Now that some (Pentecostals) are returning to the mainline churches, it shows either that the initial intention has selfish tendencies or that there are some terms of liturgy, faith experiences, and theology in the mainline that cannot be compromised.

There is need to articulate a model of Church that will explicate theologically, and ecclesiology, the reality of the Christian faith in the contemporary society, capable of making the encounter between God and humanity an experimental reality. I humbly appreciate this piece and recommend it for publishing.

The Rt. Revd. Dr. J. Akin Atere,
Bishop, Diocese of Awori & Old Testament Scholar

This examination of the influence of Mainline Churches on the Pentecostal Movement in Nigeria draws on a rich history of the church. Clearly, the mutual influence of these two streams of Christian spirituality has enriched both as they have discovered new expressions of faith and the richness of traditions once scorned.

Adewole's call for Orthodoxy and unity while drawing together traditional and innovation forms of Christian Mission is refreshing in an increasingly polarized world.

Richard Giesken
Associate Professor,
Nazarene Theological College
Thornlands, Australia.

The beauty of life is its ability to reinvigorate and adapt to changes and development in time and space as necessary. The publication was indeed a product of need when it appeared the warmth in true Christian worship was at its lowest ebb. Pentecostalism was the reawakening tool that spurred the church back to a new height. As path crossed, orthodoxy subsequently had to change her values with a view to keep afloat.

The author has been precise in bringing to light the past and the present thus projecting the new in what we are going to see as the future. For students of Church History and Religious Studies, the book is worth reading as it will stimulate interest in what we have as the developments. I hereby recommend the book for all in the field of Humanities.

Venerable Professor Taiye Aluko
Rector,
Crowther Graduate Theological Seminary,
Abeokuta

This book presents a fascinating analysis of the interconnectedness between the Mainline and Neo-Pentecostal churches underscoring a significant influence that Neo-Pentecostal had inadvertently hado n the Mainline churches. Yet it reveals a most interesting reverse through the impact of the Mainline churches that is becoming evident in the present operations of the Neo-Pentecostal churches.

This concept of Reverse Mission is exciting and thought – provoking. Scholars and Christians in Mission cannot afford to ignore this important project.

I warmly commend this study.

The Rt Revd Stephen Ayodeji A. Fagbemi PhD (Kent)
Bishop of Owo
Epiphany 2021

This masterpiece should be the constant companion of every under-shepherd in God's services. Most helpful is the fact that it emphasis not on method alone, but on character, passion, mode of worship and involvement of the Mainline Churches in evangelism. I have read and gripped the basic perspective of Pentecostal involvement in the Mainline Churches and have given it to the entire leadership of the Mainline Churches and Christian church in general to read.

This amazing book will help readers to overcome doubts on Pentecostalism in the Mainline churches mostly in Nigeria. This book is a neutralizer, no matter whom you are, God has a great understanding for you if only you can concentrate on reading and assimilating this gap-bridging book.

Ven. Dr. T.T. Bello,
Pastor, Teacher, and Old Testament Scholar

This book is good news, not just for the mainline denominations, but for the Pentecostal stream of Christianity. Indeed for all of us who believe in bold humility and vulnerability as healthy marks of church unity. The author presents a balanced view that progressively and intellectually expounds the continuous interplay between the historic churches and the Pentecostals. It is a win-win influence. Therefore, Nelson O. Adewole calls the two forms of Christianity to intentionally live a more Christ-centered lifestyle for the transformation of Nigeria and beyond. I highly recommend this resource for educators, teachers, pastors, and you.

Ven. Dr. Samuel A. Odubena,
Asbury Theological Seminary, Wilmore, KY, USA

CONTENTS

Dedication xi
Foreword xiii
Acknowledgements xv

Chapter 1   Introduction 1
  Historical Background 2
  Reverse Mission 6
  Mainline Churches 7
  Pentecostal Churches 8
  Understanding the Debate 9
  Conclusion 18
  Notes and References 20

Chapter 2   History of Christianity in Nigeria 25
  History of Mainline Churches 26
  African Indigenous Churches 30
  Pentecostal and Neo-Pentecostal Churches 31
  Conclusion 34
  Notes and References 35

Chapter 3   Influence of Pentecostalism on Mainline Churches:
            The Mission 38
  Prayer and Spirituality 38
  Special Spiritual Programmes 39
  Vigil 40
  Preaching God's word 40

Liturgy – Worship 41
Participation of Members in Worship and Church Life................ 42
Roles of Women in Church Ministry.................................... 43
Ministerial Formation and Training of Lay Members 44
Media and Communication... 45
Church Consciousness 46
Tithes and Offerings.. 46
Spirituality and Devotional Life..................................... 47
University Education 48
Conclusion... 49
Notes and References... 50

Chapter 4   Influence of Mainline Churches on Pentecostal
            Churches: A Reverse Mission............................. 53
Liturgy and Procession.. 54
The Clergy Vestments... 56
Use of Titles.. 57
Aesthetic and Church Building.. 58
Administrative Set-up and Hierarchy.................................. 58
Constitutionally Governed.. 59
Succession and Accountability 59
Christmas Carols 61
Pacesetter in Primary and Secondary Education 61
Conclusion... 61
Notes and References... 64

Chapter 5   Reverse Misson: Looking Backward and Forward to
            the Future... 67
Notes and References... 73

Bibliography... 75

DEDICATION

✠   ✠   ✠

This book is dedicated to Revd. Canon Michael Adewole Adesina (1941-2014), my father who trained and brought me up in the way of the Lord, and mother, Mrs. Mary Bosede Adewole-Adesina who constantly persuaded me for many years to further my studies after bagging my first degree.

FOREWORD

✠　　✠　　✠

Many people have interrogated the concept of reverse mission over the years to designate late 20th century efforts of African, Asian and Latin-American local missionaries to take the gospel back to Europe and North America and other earlier provenances of the gospel. The reverse mission's missionaries felt that Europe and North America have become post-Christian, spiritually withered and secularised such that the potency and primacy of the gospel of Christ have been weaned, and thus were in dire need of reviving them. It is giving back to them what they had earlier given out, which along the line, they had lost. Reverse mission then suggests a sense of gratitude and a historical duty to re-evangelise those who brought the gospel but do not have it at the material time.

From the African standpoint, many Pentecostal churches have taken reverse mission as part of their commitment to the Great Commission. It is not enough to romanticise the fact that the European and American missionaries among others brought the gospel to Africa, but it is equally imperative to examine if they are still in the faith they once preached and propagated to others. But the impact of reverse mission has been arguable because most Black churches in Europe and North America are mainly populated by the Blacks, many of whom went there with their African religious sensibility and idiosyncrasies. The transposability of the immigrant religious wares has helped them to continue with these congregations overseas. In addition, the economic downturn in Africa has been responsible for migration to Europe and America, at least, for greener pastures, rather than solely for evangelistic purposes.

No matter the debate surrounding reverse mission at the transnational level, Nelson Adewole creatively shifts the paradigm to examine the tension and intersection between the historic missions in Nigeria and their Pentecostal counterparts. This shift towards the Nigerian Christianscape is instructive. Just like the mainline churches demonised African religious beliefs and practices at their advent, so too did the Pentecostal churches demonise both African religious beliefs and the mainline churches. This act of demonisation at one time or the other resulted in an exodus from the mainline churches to the Pentecostal ones. But just within the century, there are obvious signs and practices that demonstrate that the Pentecostal churches have now engaged in reverse mission, by borrowing profusely from the mainline churches those things they had earlier condemned. But the borrowing is not one way: the mainline churches that had also condemned the Pentecostal brand as 'rascals on pulpit' have now made some reversal, becoming spiritual rascals too, at least, to retain their clients. This interesting intersection and dialectic between the mainline churches and their Pentecostal counterparts is what Adewole deftly conceptualised as reverse mission. It is indeed an attempt at blurring the lines that so unhelpfully demarcated and prevented some dialogue, which when viewed with an open mind, will set in motion the understanding that they all are expanding the reach of the Great Commission. It is on this basis that I highly recommend this book to students, scholars, clergy of mainline and Pentecostal churches, and the general readership.

Professor Benson Ohihon Igboin
Adekunle Ajasin University, Nigeria.

ACKNOWLEDGEMENTS

✠   ✠   ✠

I bless the Lord God Almighty who made this work a success. He has also sustained my life, family and ministry.

The contribution of Professor Benson Ohihon Igboin is inestimable; he did not only encourage the publication of this book, but also wrote the foreword. While also mentoring me at the Lagos State University, he exposed me to academic conferences: both local and international. Special thanks for virtually 'forcing' me to attend International Conference on African Pentecostalism (ICAP) and introducing me to Professor Afe Adogame of the Princeton Theological Seminary, New Jersey, Prof. Babatunde Adedibu, Provost of Redeemed Christian Bible College and other scholars of high repute. Meeting such religious scholars fired up my academic spirit.

Sincere gratitude to Dr. J. Akin Atere, Associate Professor Richard Giesken, Professor Taiye Aluko, Dr. Stephen Ayodeji A. Fagbemi, Dr. T.T. Bello, and Dr. Samuel A. Odubena for reading through my work and also for their suggestions and endorsements.

I thank my Bishop and wife; The Rt. Revd. Dr. J. Akin and Mrs. FolusoAtere for ever supporting my family and ministry. May you both be blessed beyond measure and be fulfilled in your episcopate.

I continue to grow in gratitude to the peaceful and loving members of the Cathedral Church of St. James, Ipate-Oyinbo, Otta (Church of Nigeria, Anglican Communion) for their understanding ever since we became their pastor. Special thanks to Ven. Ebenezer & Mrs. Shade Adewole, Revd.Samson & Mrs. Adelola Asaolu, Revd. Bukunmi & Mrs.

Lola Oniosun, Revd. Sola & Mrs. Tope Asaolu, my co-labourers in the vineyard, and Abiye Ayeyemitan who assisted in collating the scripts.

I thank Ven. Emmanuel Taiwo and Mrs. Ruth Olapeju Asaolu, my in-laws and one of the finest pastors and wife I ever met, for their ceaseless prayers, counsel and good wishes. May you enjoy longevity and robust health even in retirement.

Grace Olubunmi, my wife deserves exceptional gratitude for her strong and persuasive enthusiasm for my writing and her readiness to combine her busy professional schedule-cum-domestic roles to make my foray into academic almost seamless. Her virtue of love, care, and no dull moment keep the family warm. Accept my love and gratitude.

Finally, I appreciate the eagle eyes of Bamisope and Feyisekemi (last born), who used to read my script and encouraged me to complete the work. Omowunmi, EriOluwa, Kasopef'Oluwa and Mosopef'Oluwa all prayed for my success and willingly followed me to some research sites while on holidays. You are all blessed abundantly.

Soli Deo Gloria.

CHAPTER ONE

INTRODUCTION

✠ ✠ ✠

Since the advent of Pentecostalism in Nigerian, the Nigerian religioscape has never been the same again. The home grown and foreign mission Pentecostal churches brought massive influence on the mainline churches. This has received a great number of attentions in the public sector and academic circles. The mainline of historic churches were thoroughly sized up and criticized by leaders of the home grown and the missioners of the imported Pentecostal churches. It thereafter became a loud and wide criticism from all and sundry in the Pentecostal circle. The failures, weaknesses and excesses of the mainline churches were blown beyond proportion. Derogatory words were used for the mainline churches, like 'dead church', 'worldly church', 'lethargic church' and 'sleeping church'. The criticism gave a wide sense of consciousness to the perceived ills in the mainline churches and consequent attempts to appraise their public image and idiosyncrasies. The self-examinational exercise within the mainline churches brought about revivalism and contextualization of their doctrines, traditions and practices. This led to a better packaged, Africanised and Pentecostal form of some mainline churches. It is widely believed that the mainline churches became better off due to the influence of Pentecostalism. However, this study is a paradigm shift from the *status quo* as it examines the mostly silent influence of the mainline churches on Pentecostal churches. The research espouses the impact of the mainline churches that gave birth to the Pentecostal churches in Nigeria. The work was built on reverse mission as its theoretical framework. Practices and traditions earlier criticized are being adopted today in a growing manner that calls for attention. I will adduce reasons for the appreciation and acceptance of initially demonized practices and traditions. I will also deploy phenomenological methodology to carry out a comprehensive research, and then conclude that the mainline churches' practices and traditions over the years have been tested and proven to be Biblical and just, and as such should not be immediately repudiated, condemned or denounced. Concerted efforts should be made over time to understand why some practices and traditions are tenaciously held especially in the mainline churches from inception. The usage of the borrowed robes from either side should be studied and well understood for the right and proper adoption. Rather, mutual borrowing of good and enduring traditions would engender ecumenism and brotherliness under one God who is the Father of all.

At this introductory chapter, I shall briefly explain the background of the study, the purpose of the study, limitations and scope of the study. This becomes important so that we can be clear about the direction of this book from the outset.

Historical Background

The Christian Church grew out of apostolic traditions based on Biblical orientation and has over the years sustained her doctrines, traditions and practices. However, at a stage, reasons were given by some members and leaders of prayer groups and charismatic members to secede and start different movements.

The mainline churches were said to be too cold spiritually, worldly, stereotyped, too liturgical and regimented. The Pentecostals wanted the type of Christianity that would lay emphasis on the work of the Holy Spirit and spiritual gifts. They wanted to experience miracles, healing deliverance, signs, wonders and power encounter[1]. It became obvious that they needed to start their own movements to properly express their Christian faith. Asamoah-Gyadu referred to the earliest Pentecostals as "many of whom walked out of existing historic mission churches in order to give active expression to their new-found experiential religion"[2].

Many other reasons could be adduced for the birth of Pentecostalism in Nigeria. Pentecostalism was widely accepted by many Christians. Its impact truly shook the mainline churches to their foundations. It also proliferated and has shown phenomenal growth all over Africa and particularly in Nigeria. But lately, it has been observed that some practices and traditions that were initially criticised, derided and demonized by the Pentecostal churches are finding their ways into the Nigerian Pentecostal circle.

Pentecostalism has three basic theologies of *soteriology, Christology and pneumatology*[3]. Elijah and some charismatic leaders of Israel manifested the move of the Spirit of God in the Old Testament. Equally in the New Testament the move of the Spirit of God manifested in the life and ministry of Jesus Christ. This was extended to the apostolic era. Pentecostal phenomenon was obvious in the writings of the early Church Fathers[4]. The manifestation of the Holy Spirit was visible in the expansion of the Christian faith, in healing, prophecy, speaking in tongues and power for evangelism.

However, Pentecostalism has a firm and modern root at the beginning of the 20th century. At Bethel Bible College, Kansas, United States, Agnes Ozman was said to have spoken in tongues at the laying on of hands of the Principal of the school Charles Fox Parham (1873-1929) on January 1, 1901. Also in Los Angeles, California, Christians throughout the city were praying for an outpouring of the Holy Spirit and revival broke out in the spring of 1906. The Azusa Street Revival was a historic Pentecostal revival meeting led by William J. Seymour, an African American preacher. It began with a meeting on April 9, 1906, and it received global attention, a legacy that extends to the present day. The revival was characterized by ecstatic spiritual experiences accompanied by claims of physical healing, miracles, dramatic worship services and speaking in tongues[5].

In Nigeria, we allude to the fact that Pentecostalism predated the widely publicized 1930 revival. Garrick Sokari Braide (1882-1918) was the story of an unsung hero[6]. Olofinjana wrote that Braide is one of the pioneers of revival not just Nigeria, but in Africa. According to him,

Braide was born in Obonoma, a small Kalabari village in the Niger Delta. The village was noted as one of the leading places of traditional worship and pilgrimage in Nigeria. His parents were traditional worshippers and very poor; therefore Braide did not have the opportunity of Western education. He later became a Christian and was baptized on January 23rd 1910 at St Andrews Anglican Church in Bakana. He was noted for his enthusiasm and religious devotion. He felt called by the Lord into ministry and was accepted as a lay preacher in the Anglican Church of the Niger Delta pastorate. Braide adopted a more practical approach and contextualized the Gospel among the Delta people. He taught the people to renounce their gods, destroy their fetishes and to simply believe in the Lord Jesus he organized a crusade against charms, idol worshipping and the use of fetish objects[7].

It is widely believed that Braide's methods of ministry redefined Christianity as a practical religion for the people of the Niger-Delta, and the result was a large number of conversions to the Anglican Church. He demonstrated the gift of healing through prayer; he was believed to be a prophet called and commissioned by God. Many of his kinsmen got converted and set on fire their fetishes and charms. He stopped people from offering sacrifices and worshipping other gods. Through Braide's ministry and miracles that attended it, many people no longer visit medicine men and witch doctors.

There came a period of interaction between home grown or indigenous Pentecostal forms called *Aladura* (meaning prayer warrior) and the Faith Tabernacle from the United States of America and the Apostolic Church from Britain. Pentecostalism began to grow across Nigeria like a wild fire. Many individuals came up with visions of divine call to preach the Gospel and deliver the people from oppressions. Different forms of Pentecostalism grew from this period till date. Some place more emphasis on holiness, other neo-Pentecostals emphasised on prosperity Gospel and faith[8].

After the 16th century attempt to introduce Christianity to Nigeria through Warri and Benin by the Portuguese Catholic missionaries and the Capuchin fathers failed, the mainline churches actually re-introduced sustained Christianity to Nigeria in the 19th century[9]. This was done by the Church Missionary Society (CMS), the Weslayans (Methodists), Roman Catholic Mission (RCM), the American Baptists and Presbyterian Mission, precisely around 1842 through Badagry, Lagos, Abeokuta and Calabar. They gradually moved to the hinterland and spread widely. It is popularly asserted that Protestantism and Roman Catholicism came with a great measure of Western importation[10].

It is believed that mainline churches actually spread in Nigeria, with benefits that came with the westernized form of Christianity. However, when Pentecostalism made its way to the Nigeria religious space, there were all sorts of revival, secession and new Pentecostal church groups emerged.

As a result of the Pentecostal vivacious style of worship, emphasis on demons, witchcraft and the contextualisation of Christianity to the Nigerian milieu, there was an influx of mainline church members to the Pentecostal churches. Pentecostal leaders were also believed to have condemned and demonised virtually everything about the mainline churches. It is however surprising recently to note a reverse mission, in other words, a current paradigm shift of the Pentecostal churches imbibing some of the traditions and practices they had earlier condemned, derided and demonised.

Our work probes into those germane issues of the influence of the mainline churches on the Pentecostal churches. We are using the theoretical framework of reverse mission to bring such to limelight. Reverse Mission was first used to denote the idea of the missionaries and pastors from former mission fields now ministering to Europe and North America. Matthew Ojo, an African church historian and theologian defines reverse mission as:

> the sending of missionaries to Europe and North America by churches and Christians from the non-Western world, particularly Africa, Asia and Latin America which were at the receiving end of Catholic and Protestant missions as mission field from the sixteen century to the late twentieth century[11].

Reverse mission as far as our work is concerned is the current influence of the mainline churches on the Pentecostal churches that earlier had wielded a strong and massive influence at inception on the mainline churches. There are areas of initial Pentecostal churches' repulsion and outright rejection, now becoming part of their new practices. It is widely noted that some of the mainline churches' traditions and practices have been repackaged and adopted, and some taken hook, line and sinker. There is no doubt that Pentecostal churches actually helped in reforming the mainline churches and also restoring biblical practices that were lacking or inactive in mainline churches. But we shall attempt to establish the position that the influence is not one sided, but bipartite. Therefore, the motivation for this work is to identify areas of mainline influences on Pentecostal churches. In the meantime, it is pertinent to clarify reverse mission.

Reverse Mission

Reverse Mission is multi-lateral rather than unilateral[12] and it will be used technically differently from its common understanding. The influence of Pentecostalism on the mainline churches has received wide academic attention over the years. But a recent observation reveals a reversal of the Pentecostal churches' influences on the mainline churches. In this approach, reverse mission is the reversal of the initial massive influence of Pentecostalism on Protestantism. It is widely accepted that Pentecostal churches heavily and widely penetrated the Nigerian religious space to the extent that their influence was thoroughly impactful both positively and negatively.

Some mainline churches actually caught on the atmosphere of revivalism and high spirituality for self reformation, enhanced liturgy, more spiritual faith expression and experience. It also motivated some to re-appraise their theology, which led to a balanced theology from the African viz-a-viz Nigerian perspective. This led to what we may tag Protestant Pentecostalism. This was the merging of Pentecostal spirituality with mainline traditional spirituality. Members who caught the Pentecostal fire and decided to remain in their historic churches formed Charismatic groups in their churches. For example, in the Anglican Church, the Evangelical Fellowship in the Anglican Communion (EFAC) is the nexus and replica of what major Pentecostal churches stood for. In the Roman Catholic Church, the Catholic Charismatic Renewal[13] is such a group.

Reverse mission therefore, is the reverse phenomenon of the initial influence of Pentecostal churches. Over time, noticeable reverse waves have caught our attention on the influence of mainline churches on neo-Pentecostal churches. These are the direct and indirect impact the mainline churches have on Pentecostal churches. Having their historical backgrounds from the mainline churches, they are bound to be influenced. There were clear cut initial separation and demonization of practices and traditions of their parent churches. It is widely believed that some had the ulterior motives of membership drive, finding justifiable reasons to break away or outright giving a dog a bad name. There might not even be any sound Biblical backing for the repulsive attitude to some of the traditions and practises. However, overtime the tables are turning. Some are coming back to appreciate and appropriate what they had derided and jettisoned.

Mainline Churches

Mainline churches are usually referred to the historic, established Protestant churches. They are so-called because they are thought to represent the oldest, most influential branches of Protestantism.[14] Mainline churches are usually referred to as Historic churches that directly broke away from the Roman Catholic Church from the beginning of the 16th century. They emerged as a result of the Protestant Reformation. They are historic mission Christianity established under the auspices of Western mission bodies.[15]

However, according to the Christian Association of Nigeria (CAN) grouping of churches, recognized by the Nigerian government; mainline churches are grouped as Christian Council of Nigeria (CCN).[16] They share most religious traditions and practices in common, with little variations and distinctiveness in each denomination. The mainline churches are believed to represent the oldest, most influential branches of Protestantism. They believe in the authority of the Bible as set out in the Apostles' Creed and other church Creeds. They have share common approach to social issues. The mainline denominations are, as a rule, more theologically and politically liberal. The Western mainline churches, no doubt, are currently experiencing a shift and revisionist theology. But in the mainline denominational circle are the evangelicals, mainline churches in Nigeria are usually evangelicals. The liberal posture is actually believed to have led the Western mainline churches to modernist and revisionist theology of the Bible.

In Nigeria for instance, the Anglican Church of Nigeria is evangelical, upholding the inerrancy, divine inspiration, and authority of Scripture; they emphasize the importance of a born-againexperience through faith in Christ; they encourage evangelism and the Anglican Church in Nigeria is the fastest growing Anglican and Episcopal Church in the world[17]. But the mainline denominations in the West, especially the Church of England, Anglican Communion have seen a marked decrease in church attendance and membership[18]. However, there is a current renewal at all levels of the Anglican Communion worldwide. This renewal means changes at the structural level, as a church which has become used to maintenance becomes orientated towards mission.[19]

Mainline churches as referred to in this work are largely the Anglican Church of Nigeria, and sometimes the Methodist Church Nigeria.

Pentecostal Churches

Pentecostalism is derived from Pentecost, the Jewish Feast of Weeks. The event in the Acts of the Apostles chapter two happened on that day of the feast of the weeks. As promised by Christ, the Holy Spirit descended on the Apostles, which to some is the birth of the modern church. The word 'Pentecost' is a Greek form of '*Pentecoste*' meaning 50th day[19]. The Holy Spirit came down 50 days after the resurrection of Christ.

Pentecostalism was defined by Ayegboyin is a general term used to describe the groups and sects which have traditionally placed emphasis on the speaking and receiving of certain gifts of the Spirit, such as, speaking in tongues, prophesying and healing as a sign of the baptism of the Holy Spirit[20]. The term Pentecostal thereafter refers to the Christian experience of the power of the Holy Spirit and the manifestation of the gifts of the Holy Spirit. Pentecostal churches are those churches that broke away from the mainline churches abroad, like the Assemblies of God, Baptist Church, Apostolic Church, the Apostolic Faith, Faith Tabernacle Church, and Foursquare Church. Others are African instituted or indigenous churches, like the Christ Apostolic Church, Deeper Life Bible Church, Church of the Lord (Aladura) and the Redeemed Christian Church of God (RCCG). These churches were founded in Nigeria due to perceived lethargy and non-manifestation of the works of the Holy Spirit in the lives of the baptized believers and the existing mainline churches. They agitated for and emphasize the role of the Holy Spirit in the life and mission of the church; particularly with ecstatic phenomena like prophecy, speaking-in-tongues, and deliverance from witches, seeing vision and healing. Some actually have their historical and theological foundations in the mainline churches; but broke away at a point[21]. Others are neo-Pentecostal churches, also described as the third phase of Pentecostalism in Nigeria[22]. These further broke away from the classical and indigenous Pentecostal churches. These are; The Redeemed Evangelical Mission (TREM), Rhema Church and Towers, Sword of the Spirit Ministries, Christ Embassy, House on the Rock, Daystar Christian Centre and Mountain of Fire and Miracle Ministries.

Our reference in this study brings all of these typology and taxonomy together under the umbrella of Pentecostal churches

Understanding the Debate

Many scholars have written on diverse areas of this research. I will now explore areas of past interest that relate to aspects of this work, as well as current scholarship.

Asaju posited that Pentecostalism as a terminology is not limited to the group of Christians who are called Pentecostals.[23] We totally agreed with his stand that since Pentecostalism took its root from the Biblical account in Acts of the Apostles chapter two, the day of Pentecost and the baptism of the Holy Spirit was experienced by the early church and on the basis of that, whosoever is a Christian and who manifests these gifts is a Pentecostal irrespective of his denominational affiliation. In other words, our definition of Pentecostalism must cut across denominational delineation. Our work explores this emerging paradigm shift of the new definition of Pentecostalism, and a departure from the popular opinion scholars have held.

Moris has described Benson Idahosa as the father of Nigerian Pentecostalism.[24] However, a critical study of the history of Pentecostalism in Nigeria revealed many personalities before Idahosa that could be so described. Garrick Sokari Braide (1882-1918) could be called the father of Nigerian Pentecostalism with his exploit in the Niger-Delta area of Nigeria. Braide's ministry witnessed the demonstration of the power of the Holy Spirit in signs, wonders and miracles.[25] Many people were converted and no longer visit medicine men and witch doctors. It was a great beginning of a global phenomenon in Nigeria. Idahosa may perhaps be described as the father of neo-Pentecostalism in Nigeria.

More so, the revival of Pentecostalism in Nigeria was witnessed also around the same time in 1918, when the sexton of the St. Saviour Anglican Church, Ijebu-Ode, had dream which later led to the establishment of a prayer band to intercede for the church. The group raised Pentecostal evangelists like J. B. Sadare, David Ogunleye Odubanjo, and crop of individuals in the Precious Stone Society later renamed Diamond Society.[26]Abodunde, while assessing the making of Pentecostalism in Nigeria posited that Pentecostal explosion in Nigeria in the early years of the 20th century gave birth to many great Pentecostal evangelists and itinerant preachers, the likes of Joseph Ayo Babalola who was an early Pentecostal leader; born by Anglican parents.[27] He was at the centre stage in July 1930 when a revival broke out in Ilesa.[28]

Harold Turner later observed that the revival they sought was to come through the famous and charismatic prophet figure in the *aladura* movement, Joseph Babalola.[29] The 1930 revival saw many idol worshippers converted to the Pentecostal faith, divine healing and diverse miracles were performed, and even the resuscitation of a dead boy after Babalola offered prayers.[30] There were healing evangelists and preachers in Yorubaland like J. A. Medaiyese, Odubanjo, Akinyele, David Babajide and Peter Olatunji.[31] Also prominent among the earlier Pentecostal missionaries in 1937 was Sydney Elton from England. Elton Pentecostal mission work spanned for

50 years before his death in 1987.[32] Therefore, Morris was not fair to the above earlier Pentecostal leaders by arguing that Benson Idahosa is the father of Pentecostalism in Nigeria. Idahosa emerged in the Nigerian Pentecostal space after his ordination into ministry in 1971.[33] This work is to set the record straight as far as the history of Pentecostalism is concerned in Nigeria.

We agree with Harper who did not see Pentecostalism as a new and 20th century phenomenon; it has been with the church from inception. But when things are going bad it is only natural to want to start all over again.[34] At inception, the Pentecostal spirit came and has been present in the church. We allude to the fact that the church was established by the power of the Holy Spirit, and grew by the same power. Sadly at a time, spiritual gifts did finally disappear from the pages of church history.[35] The love of many Christians "waxed cold",[36] which led to an increasingly institutionalized church. The church became suspicious of anything that could not be rationally explained. Speaking in tongues, for example, was treated as evidence of demon-possession. The healing ministry of the church virtually disappeared too at this time. However, during Reformation, some of these gifts resurfaced.[37]

Towards the end of the 19th century as alluded to above, many Christians began to pray for revival. The revival actually broke out. This was facilitated by some Christian groups that were really expectant: The "Holiness Movement", The Salvation Army and the Keswick Convention Movement.[38] Our work traces the root from Asuza Street and the Nigerian Pentecostal revival in the early 20th century.

Ward opined that Pentecostalism is a challenge to Anglicans in all parts of Africa.[39] He felt Pentecostalism greatly affected the Anglican youths in Africa and has led to their movement out of the Anglican Church, especially when they are not open to charismatic form of Christianity. What Ward did not construe is that Pentecostalism is not a challenge to the Anglicans alone, but to other mainline churches. Also that the challenge of Pentecostalism extends beyond Africa. It is a disporic and global one. Napolitano in his work on African Pentecostalism in Italy concluded that it was an entangled history of religion and state, and that one can trace the painful history of Italian Pentecostalism.[40] Pentecostalism in Italy and some Catholic dominated European countries is a serious challenge to the Roman Catholic church and the government.

Butticci, while writing about Pentecostalism and the Italian government alluded to a government ruling in 1935 that ordered that all prefectures all over Italy outlawed Pentecostal gatherings.[41] The order defined Pentecostal gathering as religious practices contrary to the social order and harmful to the physical and psychological intLLergrity of the race.[42] To this extent, Ward's argument is incomplete as it focused on Anglicans alone. Therefore, our work researched into how Pentecostalism has made impact on other mainline churches.

Abodunde in his work on the history of Pentecostalism in Nigeria expatiated on a period in the middle of the 20th century when Pentecostalism experienced a global slowdown and dryness.[43] He further noted that services and preaching became ritualized. Abodunde did not investigate into reasons that caused such stagnation. Our work probes into such reasons and also discovered that it was a similar experience in the mainline churches that brought about Pentecostal revival of the early years of the 20th century.

Larbi made an interesting summary of his phenomenological study of the African Pentecostalism. He opined that Pentecostal movements derived power and success from its solidarity with the poor. He further stated that Pentecostals believe in secret intercessory prayer about political matters, rather than engage in politics.[44] In the Nigerian Pentecostal churches' context, this may be far from the reality. Nigerians are witnessing an era of deep involvement of many foremost Pentecostal leaders in underground and active politics. According to Laguda, the 2011 and 2015 general elections are pointers.[45] He argued that the alignments and re-alignments of the political class with Pentecostal leaders, the visits of political gladiators to prominent Pentecostal leaders, churches and camps, the prayers for political success and protection and other political intrigues were panoramic.[46] For example Dr. Goodluck Jonathan, the then President of the Federal Republic of Nigeria, who was re-contesting and Muhammadu Buhari the popular candidate of All Progressive Congress (APC) at different times visited the Redemption Camp of the Redeemed Christian Church of God; where they were prayed for by Pastor Enoch Adeboye, the General Overseer. Goodluck Jonathan equally visited Canaanland, the headquarters of the Living Faith Church, where Bishop David Oyedepo also prayed for him. Pastor Tunde Bakare, the pastor and founder of the Latter Rain Assembly; a neo-Pentecostal church became the running mate of General

Muhammadu Buhari in 2011. In 2015, Professor 'Yemi Osibajo, a senior pastor of the popular Redeemed Christian Church of God became the vice President of Nigeria.[47] To this extent, the Pentecostal leaders and churches involvement in politics against Larbi's submission is glaring.

The submission of Larbi about Pentecostal solidarity with the poor could also be proven not to be a true survey. The emphasis on prosperity gospel has made some classical and neo-Pentecostal churches become a religious space for the rich; while pauperism, destitution and poverty are simply interpreted as God's chastisement.[48] The messages made some poor adherents to see themselves as sinners, why they are not wealthy and successful. Olalekan contended that in order to understand the new Pentecostal landscape of Nigeria as far as prosperity gospel is concerned, we must critically assess the influence of American preachers on Nigerian prosperity gospel preachers. Benson Idahosa, David Oyedepo of the Living Faith Church and others clearly state their indebtedness to their American mentors.[49] Such as Keneth E. Hagin and his Bible Training Centre, Keneth Copeland, Fredrick K. C. Price, T. L. Osborn, John L. Meares, T. D. Jakes, etc.[50]Olalekan posited that prosperity gospel preachers ask their members to give generously in exchange for material and spiritual blessings in the form of healing, wealth, abundant life, success and earthly promotion.[51] But it has been widely observed that the followers of this gospel, regarded by some scholars as "American export"[52] are rather becoming poorer with the Nigerian economic reality, while the preacher themselves live in affluence and super abundance. This raises questions about the motives of prosperity gospel preachers.

Igboin argued from the perspective of secularization and the African Pentecostalism in investigating the Pentecostal prosperity gospel. According to him,

> There is usually a complex mix when one relates secularization to African Pentecostalism. This is partly because the historiographical accounts of many Pentecostal churches clearly underscore the fact that they started in America from where the dose of mundanity that has become a kind of spiritual albatross today on many of them was incubated.[53]

His argument corroborates the fact that prosperity gospel was imported to the Nigerian Pentecostal space due to the foreign influence of the American preachers. This argument was further stressed by Adedibu who posited that three cardinal thrusts could have led to the emergence and influence of prosperity theology of the American Pentecostalism. According to him, they are experience-based epistemology influenced by the religious thoughts of Fredrich Schleiermacher; the pervasive principle and praxis of American health and wealth theology anchored on Norman Vincent Peale's positive philosophy; and suffusing Western materialism.[54] Igboin alluded to the fact that these three waves of Pentecostalism's emergence can be situated within the spectrum of capitalism and avarice for 'worldliness.[55]

Therefore, alluding to the above opinions and the argument of Olalekan that African Pentecostals, viz-a-viz the Nigerian version now compete favourably with the contemporary world.[56] Pentecostalism in the Nigerian religious space could not be really said to be in solidarity with the poor.

Kitause posited that Pentecostalism today is a universal phenomenon; it is no longer a Pentecostals' affairs only, but the mainstream Christians experience as well.[57] Smart also agreed in totality with this standpoint, he argued that modern Christianity has shaped itself more and more in ways that cut across denominational and organizational lines.[58] Thus the ecstatic Biblicism of Pentecostals can be found outside groups that label themselves as such. In other words, Pentecostal life is now evident in the lives of Christians of all persuasions within the Nigerian religious firmament.

Asaju on the current trends in Pentecostalism posited that denominational barriers are being crossed.[59] Pentecostalization[60] was used by Gyadu in an attempt to describe the survival strategy of the mainline churches at the time when they were experiencing massive defection to the Pentecostal churches. The main reason for such exodus in the perspective of the defectors was to find spiritual nourishment from Pentecostal churches. This makes the mainline churches to mellow down to accommodate Pentecostal practices. This was an effort to create an enabling environment for the departing members to stay back in the Church. This strategy is what Gyadu called the 'Pentecostalization' of the mainline churches. Our work alluded to the position that the definitions of Pentecostalism have crossed denominational delineations and barriers. In other words, many mainline churches have been pentecostalized.

Pentecostal churches as well as mainline churches are faced with the challenge of exclusiveness, which according to Umejesi and Igboin is an ideology that brackets out traditions which are not one's own as false.[61] Both streams of Christianity are mutually beneficial. The influence of Pentecostalism has enhancedworship in the mainline churches and contextualized the westernized Christianity to meet the African zeal, vivacious nature and cosmology.

Kalu while commenting on the influence of Pentecostalism on the mainline churches said it caused much stir among them and strategies were quickly put in place to map out counter-insurgence or to formulate policy on damage control measures.[62] These counter-insurgence strategies and damage control measures made many mainline churches to become charismatic and Pentecostal; these are issues to be addressed in our work.

Zink in his work on what he coined as 'Anglocostalism' in Nigeria explored how the initial policies of exclusion and rejection evolved into accommodation and imitation.[63] He further aptly posited:

> That worship has changed; there is a greater emphasis on healing, an increased recognition of a supernatural world, a tendency towards seeing the world in binary terms, more common references to prosperity gospel theology, and a different understanding of the authority of the Bible. These changes amount to a profound re-shaping of Anglicanism in the Nigerian context.[64]

Zink revealed how Pentecostalism has influenced the Anglican Church. He cited examples of some areas of the influence to buttress his claim and drive home the message. These include: ethics and church liturgy, preaching of good homilies, singing of choruses after the manner of the Pentecostals, copied the flamboyant life style of the Pentecostals. Also, they now urge people to pay tithe instead of voluntary offering done out of love for God and in support of His church. They seem not to value their Anglican identity and theology. Some priests now shy away from saying the collects and litany. Evil spirits or demon possession has gained currency among Anglicans as a result of Pentecostal emphasis on it. Zink's view is clear and penetrating in showing that Pentecostalism cannot be wished away in the mainline churches' perspective of Christianity today in Nigeria.

We allude to the opinion that the current rise of neo-Pentecostal churches and their emphasis on prosperity gospel, focus on spiritual warfare and deliverance, love for African gospel music and charismatic worship style have changed the face of Anglicanism and other mainline churches in Nigeria. Zink observed that the concern about the possibility of diminished influence and prestige has made the Anglican Church to respond by adopting more of its rivals' beliefs and practices.[65] In other words, Anglicans and other mainline churches in Nigeria have responded to the rapid growth of neo-Pentecostal churches by adopting attributes of those churches. The result has been significant changes to traditional patterns of worship, belief, and doctrine that have made Anglicans more like the neo-Pentecostal churches. These are the influence of Pentecostalism on the mainline churches which our work addresses.

McGrath harping on the need for renewal of Anglicanism pleaded that the dereliction of the Anglican heritage must not be allowed to happen, he expressed the hope that both western Christianity and the universal church will be enriched by the continuing presence of an Anglicanism within its ranks which is as self-confidence as it is self-critical.[66]We agree with McGrath in his opinion as it is vital for Anglicans to cherish and preserve their traditions and practices. Not just for self-sustenance and originality, but to have a legacy to enrich other Christian churches. It is believed that Anglicanism has a contribution to make to the universal church.

Reverse mission, our theoretical framework in studying the influence of mainline churches on Pentecostal churches is gradually becoming a phrase in academia, mission circles, and among Christians from the 'two-thirds world'.[66] It explains the missionary strategy by churches in Africa, Asia and Latin America of re-evangelizing the 'West'. The enterprise was aimed at re-Christianising Europe and North America in particular, the former heartlands of Christianity and vanguards of missionary movements from the sixteenth to the twentieth century.[67]

Olupona argued in favour of the trend of reverse mission from the perspective of several African ministers in Europe, America and other western countries that Africa has become one of the centres of Christianity and is ripe enough to send missionaries abroad.[68]Reverse mission postulated that Christianity was rising rapidly in the global South and missionary activity was now beginning to flow back in the opposite direction to that which had characterized the previous 200 to 300 years.[69]

Adogame argued that:

> The rationale for reverse mission is often anchored on claims to divine commission to 'spread the gospel'; the perceived secularization of the West; the abysmal fall in church attendance and dwindling membership; desecralisation of church buildings; liberalization; and on issues around moral decadence.[70]

The punch here is that due to the failure of the western Christianity alluded to above; the Christendom is currently witnessing the export of Christianity to the earlier missionaries' domain. Adogame argued further that;

> Nonetheless, reverse mission as 'rhetoric' or 'an evolving process' is of crucial religious, social, political, economic and missiological import for the 'West' and the global church, as the nonwestern world were hitherto at the receiving end of missions till the late twentieth century. The emergence of the 'global South' as the new centre of gravity of Christianity provides the watershed for the reversal and/or multidirectionality of missions.[71]

The emerging paradigm shift is paradoxical and unbelievable. But the reality is what scholarship needs to grapple with.

The usage in this work is a departure from the popular parlance. Reverse mission as technically used in our work argues that there is currently a departure from the common scholarship of a one-sided influence of Pentecostal churches on mainline churches. In other words, we posited that overtime, mainline churches are now having heavy and obvious influences on some Pentecostal churches.

Asaju further queried the identity of the Pentecostals when many Pentecostal churches have radically returned to the vestments, the liturgies and the traditions of the mainline churches which they hitherto criticized.[72] Asaju's view captured the new trends in some neo-Pentecostal churches, although he did not give any reason why the Pentecostals are returning to those things they had earlier criticized. The reasons will be supplied in our work.

We are also unaware of the fact that some classical Pentecostal churches have been consistent on their stand about vestments, liturgies and traditions. For example, we opined that the Deeper Life Bible Church has been consistent since inception on its stand against these pertinent issues, which it considered mere religiosity. Danfulani posited that Pastor William F. Kumuyi has remained conservative.[74] The thrust of our work is to identify some of the neo-Pentecostal churches that have returned to vestments, liturgies and traditions of the mainline churches.

We have reviewed various works related to our topic and discovered commendable aspects of scholarship. We have also ascertained the activities and huge success of the mainline churches that introduced orthodox Christianity into Nigeria, although the type that did not come with answers to the questions of African cosmological challenges and powers but later woke up to the reality. Our review also revealed divine intervention to a dying faith lacking in the manifestation of the gifts and power of the Holy Spirit. The Asuza Street Pentecostal explosion brought about a global phenomenological wind of change. The Holy Spirit was welcomed back to the church universal, with a global spread and attention. Nigerian religious space was not left out as the Pentecostal wind of change blew across the land and steered up the already established mainline churches. New churches were launched and later proliferated. However, the reverse mission in intra-Christian denomination will be further investigated in the following chapters.

Conclusion

We have considered the motivation for our work, the double-sided influences of Pentecostal churches on mainline churches. We have also traced a concise international and Nigerian history of Pentecostalism as an off-shoot of the mainline Protestant churches. We have also been able to establish the fact that the mainline churches introduced Christianity into Nigeria which later prepared ground for the explosion of Pentecostalism. We equally stated the purpose of study which is pungently to investigate areas of mutual influences between the mainline and Pentecostal churches. We have deciphered the research methodology appropriate for our work. Our scope and limitation were also well stated. The chapter also included clarification of major terms used in the work.

Notes and References

1 Ezekiel O. Ajani, *"Transnational Dynamics and the Challenges of Cross Cultural Adaptation among the Mountain of Fire and Miracles Ministries in the Netherlands"*. A Paper presented at International Conference on African Pentecostalism (ICAP 2017), at The Redeemed Christian Bible College, Mowe, Nigeria 13-15 June 2017, 3.

2 Johnson Kwabena Asamoah-Gyadu, "I will Put My Breath in You, and You Will Come to Life': Charismatic Renewal in Ghanaian Mainline Churches and its Implication for Africa 'Diasporean' Christianity" in: Afe Adogame, Roswith Gerloff and Klaus Hock (eds), *Christianity in Africa and the African Diaspora* (London, New-York: Continuum International Publishing Group, 2008), 193.

3 Adepeju O. Bashua, CRS 839: Systematic and Pentecostal Theology, 2017, 43.

4 Bashua, 42.

5 http://www.apostolicarchives.com/articles/article/8801925/173190. htm (accessed July 5, 2017).

6 Israel Oluwole Olofinjana, The Story of an Unsung Hero: History and Legacy of Garrick Sokari Braide (1882-1918),https://israelolofinjana. wordpress.com/2012/01/15/the-story-of-an-unsung-hero-history-and-legacy-of-garrick-sokari-braide-1882-1918/ (accessed June 23, 2017).

7 Israel Oluwole Olofinjana, The Story of an Unsung Hero: History and Legacy of Garrick Sokari Braide (1882-1918), (accessed June 23, 2017).

8 Bashua, 47.

9 Bashua, 30.

10 Adepeju O. Bashua, CRS 827: Missiology, 2017, 32.

11 M. Ojo, "Reverse Mission", in Jonathan J. Bonk (ed.), *Encyclopedia of Mission and Missionaries,* (New York: Routledge, 2007), 380.

12 A. Adogame, *The Rhetoric of Reverse Mission: African Christianity and the changing dynamics of religious expansion in Europe*, Outline of Lecture presented at the Conference, *"South moving North: revised mission and its implications"* Protestant Landelijk Dienstencentrum, Utrecht, 26th September 2007.

13 H.C.Achunike, *Catholic Charismatic Movement in Igbo land, 1970 - 1995.*(Enugu: Fourth Dimension Publishing Company Ltd, 2009), 31.

14 Got a Question.Org, https://www.gotquestions.org/mainline-denomi nations.html, (accessed October 14, 2017).

15 Johnson Kwabena Asamoah-Gyadu, "I will Put My… 195.

16 Christian Association of Nigeria (CAN), Membership, http:// cannigeria.org/membership/ accessed 24th June, 2017.

17 Church of Nigeria, About us, https://anglican-nig.org/about-us/ accessed 24th June, 2017.

18 The Guardian Online, News, https://www.theguardian.com/ world/2016/jan/12/church-of-england-attendance-falls-below-million-first-time (accessed 24th June, 2017).

19 Alister E. McGrath, *The Renewal of Anglicanism*, (London: SPCK, 1993), 10.

20 Gabriel, N, "Influences of Pentecostalism on the Mainline Churches in Nigeria" *Archives of Business Research*, Volume 3, Number 3, (2015), 68.

21 Deji Ayegboyin and S. Ademola Ishola, *African Indigenous Churches: An Historical Perspective* (Lagos: Greater Heights Publication, 1997), 16.

22 Asaju, Dapo, Keynote address on *African Pentecostalism and development in Africa and Dispora* at International Conference of African Pentecostalism (ICAP 2017), at The Redeemed Christian Bible College, Mowe, Nigeria 13-15 June 2017.

23 Deji Ayegboyin, "Resonance of African Initiated Churches' Beliefs and Practices in Nigeria Pentecostal Praxis," *SPECTRUM Journal of Contemporary Christianity and Society*, Vol. 2, No 1 (2017): 7.

24 Dapo Asaju, Keynote address on *African Pentecostalism and Development in Africa and Dispora* at International Conference of African Pentecostalism (ICAP 2017), at The Redeemed Christian Bible College, Mowe, Nigeria 13-15 June 2017.

25 Innocent Morris, "The Biography of Archbishop Benson Idahosa" http://innocentministries.blogspot.com.ng/2013/01/biography-of-archibishop-benson-idahosa.html (accessed July 8, 2017).

26 Israel Oluwole Olofinjana, The Story of an Unsung Hero: History and Legacy of Garrick Sokari Braide (1882-1918),(accessed on July 5, 2017).

27 Ayodeji Abodunde, *Messenger: Sydney Elton and the Making of Pentecostalism in Nigeria,* (Lagos: Pierce Watershed, 2016), 29.

28 Abodunde, 31.

29 H. W. Turner, "Pentecostal Movements in Nigeria", *Orita: Ibadan Journal of Religious Studies*, Vol. 6, no. 1, (1967), 44.

30 Abodunde, 34.

31 Abodunde, 79.

32 Abodunde, 395.

33 Abodunde, 301.

34 Michael Harper, *As At The Beginning The Twentieth Century Pentecostal Revival,* (London: Hodder & Stoughton, 1965), 18.

35 Michael, 19.

36 Michael, 20.

37 Michael, 20.

38 Michael, 22.

39 Kevin Ward, "The Empire Fights Back – The Invention of African Anglicanism" in Afe Adogame, Roswith Gerloff & Klaus Hock (eds), *Christianity in Africa and the African Diaspora* (London, New York: Continuum, 2008), 92.

40 Carmine Napolitano, "The Development of Pentecostalism in Italy", in Williams Kay and Anne Dyer (eds), *European Pentecostalism* (Leiden, Neitherlands: Brill, 2011), 189-204.

41 Annalisa Butticci, *African Pentecostals in Catholic Europe– The Politics of Presence in the Twenty-First Century,* (Cambridge, London: Harvard University Press, 2016), 34.

42 Butticci, 34.

43 Abodunde, 99-100.

44 Kingsley, E. Larbi, *Pentecostalism: The Eddies of Ghanaian Christianity* (Accra: Centre for Pentecostal and Charismatic Studies, SAPC Series 1, 2001), 24.

45 Danoye Oguntola Laguda, CRS 807: Sociology of Religion, 2017, Lecture notes.

46 Laguda, Lecture notes.

47 Dairo Afolorunso Olalekan, "...Being in the World and not Part of the World" The Changing Faces of Pentecostalism in the 21st Century Nigeria" *SPECTRUM Journal of Contemporary Christianity and Society,* Vol. 2, No 1 (2017), 47.

48 Deji Ayegboyin, "New Pentecostal Churches and Prosperity Theology in Nigeria" in Afe Adogame (ed), *Who is Afraid of the Holy Ghost?*

Pentecostalism and Globalization in Africa and Beyond, (New Jersey: Africa World Press, 2011), 155.

49 Olalekan, 53.

50 Olalekan, 54.

51 Olalekan, 53

52 Olalekan, 53.

53 Benson Igboin "Secularization of African Religious Space: From Perspective to Pluriversalism" *SPECTRUM Journal of Contemporary Christianity and Society*, Vol. 2, No 1 (2017): 60.

54 Babatunde Adedibu, "God and Marmon: Piety and Probity of Britain's Black Majority Churches," *Nigerian Journal of Christian Studies*, 11 (2015), 211-212

55 Igboin, 75.

56 Olalekan, 56.

57 Rimamsikwe Habila Kitause "Influence of Pentecostalism on the Mainline Churches In Nigeria: 1970-2015" *International Journal of Humanities, Arts, Medicine and Sciences* Vol. 3, Issue 7, (July 2015): 1-10.

58 Ninian Smart, *The Phenomenon of Christianity* (London: Collins, 1979), 137.

59 Asaju, Keynote address on *African Pentecostalism and development in Africa and Dispora.*

60 J.K.A Gyadu, *African Charismatics: Current Developments within Independent Indigenous Pentecostalism in Ghana*, (Leiden: Sefer, 2005), 30.

61 Innocent Ogonna Umejesi and Benson Ohihon Igboin, "Styles and Attitudes to the Study of Religions: An Appraisal of the Nigerian Religious Universe" in Adam K. Arap Chepkwony & Peter M. J. Hess (eds), *Human Views on God: Variety Not Monotony (Essay in Honour of Ade P. Dopamu* (Eldoret: Moi University Press, 2010), 123.

62 Ogbu U. Kalu, "Who is Afraid of the Holy Ghost? Presbyterians and Early Charismatic Movement in Nigeria, 1966-1975" in Afe Adogame (ed), *Who is Afraid of the Holy Ghost?*, 83.

63 Jesse Zink,'Anglocostalism' in Nigeria: NeoPentecostalism and Obstacles to Anglican Uniy. *Journal of Anglican Studies*, Available on CJO 2012 doi:10.1017/ S1740355312000125.February 2013, 2.

64   Zink, 2.

65   Zink, 12.

66   McGrath, 10.

67   Afe Adogame, *"Reverse Mission: Europe - a Prodigal Continent?"* http://
      www.wcc2006.info/fileadmin/files/edinburgh2010/files/News/Afe_
      Reverse%20mission_edited.pdf (accessed on July 8, 2017).

68   Adogame, *"Reverse Mission: Europe* (accessed July 8, 2017).

69   Jacob Olupona, "Globalization and African Immigrant Churches in
      America" in Afe Adogame (ed), *Who is Afraid of the Holy Ghost?
      Pentecostalism and Globalization in Africa and Beyond*, (New Jersey:
      Africa World Press, 2011), 78-79.

70   Forbes, "Christianity's Reverse Mission Agenda"https://www.forbes.
      com/2010/07/17/religion-christianity-reverse-mission-opinions-
      oxford-analytica.html (accessed July 11, 2017).

71   Adogame, *"Reverse Mission: Europe* (accessed July 8, 2017).

72   Adogame, *"Reverse Mission: Europe* (accessed July 8, 2017).

73   Dapo Asaju, Keynote address on *African Pentecostalism and development
      in Africa and Dispora.*

74   Umar Habila Dadem Danfulani, "Globalization, Fundamentalism and
      the Pentecostal/Charismatic Movement in Nigeria" in Afe Adogame
      (ed), *Who is Afraid of the Holy Ghost*, 38-39.

CHAPTER TWO

HISTORY OF CHRISTIANITY IN NIGERIA

✠   ✠   ✠

T he first attempt to introduce Christianity to the geographical area later known as Nigeria was in Benin/Warri areas of Niger Delta in the 15th century. It was carried out by the Catholic Portuguese Missionaries. However, the attempt was a failure because of many reasons including language barrier, concentration for many places and high mortality rate among the missionaries.[1]

Considering the beginning of the history of Christianity in Nigeria up till date, many stages of growth had taken place. Many churches of diverse foreign and indigenous denominations have been launched and nurtured. Today it is herculean to categorize churches in typologies and taxonomies.

The Christian Association of Nigeria (CAN) lately tried to group these many denominations into five blocs[2] viz-a-viz Christian Council of Nigeria (CCN), Catholic Secretariat of Nigeria (CSN), Christian Pentecostal Fellowship of Nigeria (CPFN) /Pentecostal Fellowship of Nigeria (PFN), Organization of African Instituted Churches (OAIC) and lastly the *Tarayar Ekklesiyoyin Kristi a Nigeria* (TEAKAN, The Fellowship of the Churches of Christ in Nigeria) and Evangelical Church Winning All (ECWA) Fellowship. Each church knows where it belongs. For instance, the Anglican Church, Methodist Church and other mainline churches belong to the CCN, the classical and neo Pentecostal churches belong to the CPFN/PFN and the various white garment churches belong to the OAIC bloc.

However, for the purpose of our work we shall consider the historiography of Christianity in Nigeria in three different phases. These three phases will reveal the history of churches in Nigeria.

History of Mainline Churches

The European Christian missionaries however made a second attempt to introduce Christianity to Nigeria in the 19th century. The phase was led by the Methodist mission in September, 1842 under the leadership of Thomas Birch Freeman.[3] He entered Abeokuta through Badagry which became an entreport to Yorubaland. He was followed closely by Henry Townsend, a missionary of the Church Missionary Society (CMS), who equally settled in Abeokuta in December, 1842.[4] These earlier missionaries were followed by the American Baptist missionaries in 1850 and Roman Catholicism through the Society of the African Mission in 1862 in the evangelization of Nigeria. The Christian missionaries equally visited the Eastern part of Nigeria almost at the time they visited Yorubaland. The Presbyterian missionaries became succesful in 1858[5] and the Qua Iboe Mission in 1887.[6] The Christian missionary enterprise was delayed in the northern part of the country because of religious and political factors.[7] However, mission work started in northern Nigeria in 1893. The Sudan United Mission (SUM) joined the Sudan Interior Mission (SIM) in the mission work in the north.[8]

This phase was portrayed by missionary activities being based on denominations. The language barrier was reduced to the barest minimum by the use of interpreters. The missionaries themselves learned the Nigerian languages. Converts were taught how to read and write. The children too were brought to school for education; this became an effective way of making converts of the children.[9] Trained Nigerian ministers started to come forward. Churches, schools and hospitals were built. Converts were baptized as a Christian practice and an unforgetable mark for the new faith they had received and the old ways they had abandoned. High moral standards were also taught and enforced in mission schools.

The role of the liberated slaves in the spread of Christianity in Nigeria cannot be overempasized during this era. After the abolition of slave trade by the Abolition Act of 1807, the freed slaves of Nigerian descent had settled in Freetown, Sierra Leone. They began to travel to Lagos and Badagry for trading purpose. The Yoruba began to make communal efforts to regain contact with their relations. In 1830, some Yoruba from Freetown travelled to their home towns to unite with their people. Some of them who had become Christians requested for missionaries to come and establish mission stations in their towns. Such move really facilitated the spread of Christianity. Credence must be given to the activities of missionaries like Revd. Henry Townsend, Revd. Thomas Birch Freeman, Revd. Samuel Ajayi Crowther (later Bishop), and a host of others.

Methodist Church Nigeria, a prominent mainline church is arguably the oldest church denomination in the country.[10] Revd Thomas Birch Freeman; the first Methodist minister to as stated earlier, arrived Nigeria on September 24, 1842. An Anglo-African missionary, he fought several personal battles including the loss of a dear wife to step foot in Badagry. He made up his mind to spread the good news of salvation through Jesus Christ. He became successful after many years of his mission work together with other missionaries who later joined him. The efforts of the Methodist missionaries included the establishment of Wesley Guild Hospital, Ilesha, Royal Cross Methodist Hospital, School of Nursing, and a Motherless Babies Home all in Uzuakoli, Abia State. Many other hospitals of international standard and a School of Health Technology were established. In the field of education, Freeman and other missionaries established schools alongside the preaching of the gospel, beginning with a nursery school in Badagry in 1842. They proceeded from that foundation level to a secondary and teachers' training colleges with aid from overseas churches.

One of the duties of mission schools was to build high moral standards and characters besides giving education which is why most of the people trained by the mission schools had sound moral and capacity development training which stood them out in their various chosen careers. Even with the government takeover of schools, Methodist Church Nigeria now has 95 nursery and primary schools and 72 secondary schools in different parts of the country.[11] Wesley University of Science and Technology,

Ondo was founded by the Methodist Church Nigeria in 2007[12] to further show that the church values the role of education in the development of Nigeria. Spiritually and administratively, the Methodist Church Nigeria is headed by the prelate, who presides over the conference, the overall governing body of the church. This conference meets every two years to deliberate and take decisions on all issues affecting the life of the church. The conference area is divided into eight archdioceses. Each archdiocese is composed of not less than four dioceses over which an archbishop presides at the archdiocesan council meetings. There are 44 dioceses. On church growth, from the mission stations established in Badagry and Abeokuta, the Methodist church spread to various parts of the country west of the River Niger and part of the north. Today there are over 2000 congregations and over 2,000,000 members in Nigeria.[13] Methodist Church Nigeria and the Anglican Church in Nigeria share similar doctrines and traditions. It is believed by many that both have also been Pentecostalized with the influence of Pentecostalism. They also have a joint seminary; Immanuel College of Theology[14], Ibadan where priests are trained for the two mainline churches.

The growth of the Church of Nigeria (Anglican Communion) since the end of the Slave Trade has been a very rapid one. It is interesting to know that within two centuries, Christianity and indeed Anglicanism, which started quietly in Badagry and Abeokuta has spread like wild fire to all nooks and crannies of Nigeria. In 1842, Revd Henry Townsend of the Church Missionary Society sowed the seed of Anglicanism when he landed in Badagry from Freetown, Sierra Leone. After the ordination of the Revd. Henry Townsend and the Revd. Samuel Ajayi Crowther in England in 1842, they both returned to Abeokuta.[15] With the untiring efforts of these evangelists, many Nigerians were converted to Christianity. On December 25, 1842 in Abeokuta, Nigerians were able to celebrate for the very first time, the glorious annunciation that the Saviour, who is Christ the Lord, was born.[16] They gave glory to God Almighty, experiencing the peace and joy of the Lord; Anglicanism had been born in Nigeria. In 1846, the Revd. Samuel Ajayi Crowther, the Revd. Henry Townsend, in company the Revd. Colmer and Mr. Phillips worked together to consolidate the CMS Yoruba Mission. In 1857, the Revd. Samuel Ajayi Crowther led the CMS Niger Mission to Onitsha and environs to found a formidable native pastorate.[17]

Revd. Samuel Ajayi Crowther was elected Bishop in 1864 and posted to the See of the Niger. Anglicanism soon had a secure base in Lagos, which became a Diocese on December 10, 1919 with F. Melville Jones as Bishop and Isaac Oluwole, Assistant Bishop.[18] When Leslie Gordon Vining succeeded Jones as Bishop of Lagos in 1940, the Anglican Church in Nigeria had a new vista opened. By 1955 when he died at sea, Vining, the last "white" Bishop of Lagos and the first Archbishop of the Province of West Africa had taken giant strides to expand the frontiers of the Anglican Church and training scores of young and dynamic Nigerian priests.

The thirty-nine Articles of Religion are the basic doctrines of the Anglican Church. These are various confessional statements rooted in scripture for a proper defence of the authentic Christian faith.[19] The Articles are meant to keep the Anglican Church within the confines of the apostolic faith and also to prevent it from slipping into the heretical teaching of any generation. The relevance of the scriptures to the Anglicans cannot be overemphasized. Traditions and reason are veritable tools for perfect understanding of the scriptures to the Anglicans.[20] Today the Anglican Church in Nigeria has not only grown so wide to every nook and cranny of Nigeria, but it is the fastest growing Anglican and Episcopal Church in the world.[21] There are currently 13 Ecclesiastical Provinces in the Church of Nigeria with the headquarters in Abuja, each comprising at least 8 dioceses. In all, there are 167 dioceses including 3 in the United States of America and Canada to cater for Nigerian Anglicans as protection from the western revisionist agenda, especially on human sexuality.[22] The Anglican Church of Nigeria is currently led by the Primate of All Nigeria, the Most Revd. Nicholas Dikeriehi Orogodo Okoh and other bishops, each in their Dioceses. The General Synod meets every three years to take decisions about the church and in between the period the Standing Committee meets twice yearly to control and enforce the decisions of the General Synod.[23]

The missionaries were succesful in the western and eastern Nigeria, they also made impact in the northern Nigeria. Churches, schools and hospitals were opened across the length and breath of Nigeria. They played major role in the Nigerian national development. The area of training and education for their converts and workers were well handled. Health care and commerce were also scaled up.[24]

African Indigenous Churches

The second phase of the history of Christianity in Nigeria is the emergence of Aladura or African Indegenous Churches (AICs). This group according to CAN bloc grouping is the OAIC. The Aladura movement in many ways can be referred to as the fore-runner of the classical Pentecostal churches in Nigeria. The Aladura movement started what is today known as Pentecostalism in Nigeria. The Nigerian Pentecostalism traced its root to the history of the Aladura movement. The Aladura movement's history could be traced to the activities of Garrick Braide, an Anglican Catechist in the Niger-Delta area of Nigeria in 1915,[25] which we have earlier narrated also as the root of Nigerian Pentecostalism in this work. The prophetic-healing movement led by J. B. Sadare at St. Saviour's Anglican Church, Ijebu-Ode was also another root of the Aladura movement[26].

According to Fatokun, the third acknowledged prophetic-healing movement to surface in the history of Nigerian Pentecostalism is the Cherubim and Seraphim Society founded in Lagos in 1925 by Moses Orimolade an indigene of Ikare-Akoko, and a fifteen-year old girl, Christiana Abiodun Akinsowon.[27] Another prophetic-healing movement of indigenous character is the Church of the Lord (Aladura) founded in 1930 at Ogere, by Josiah Oluwalowo Oshitelu, a teacher and Catechist of the Anglican Church.[28]

The African Indigenous Churches grew out of both backgrounds of African traditional heritage and the western or mission initiated churches.[29] They absorbed some of the cherished beliefs and practices of those traditions. Aladura in Yoruba means praying people or practitioners of prayer. Fatokun commented on the term thus:

> By historical origin, the term Aladura was a Yoruba coinage given in Yorubaland by the Yoruba speaking people as a pejorative label to the first prophetic-healing Pentecostal movement that emerged in South-western Nigeria.[30]

Early Aladura churches include the Eternal Sacred Order of the Cherubim and Seraphim Society, founded in 1925, and the Church of the Lord (Aladura), founded around 1929. Christ Apostolic Church,

(C.A.C.) by Joseph Ayo Babalola, and Celestial Church of Christ (C.C.C.) founded by Samuel Oshoffa. These were indigenous Churches founded by Nigerians. According to Akin Omoyajowo, "the Aladura churches are churches which began the indigenous churches, founded by indigenous persons, and run under indigenous leadership".[31]

The Aladura churches combined the two fundamental elements of Christianity and African culture, in a way that advertised their Christian intentions without undermining their African credentials. They emphasized some features which are relevant and valued by the African people, such as, prophecy, healing, prayer, vision, dream and the use of sacred objects[32]. Within some years of existence, most especially, between 1920's-1960's, the Aladura Churches grew phenomenally in the nooks and crannies of Yorubaland and beyond. Different scientific and technological strategies of preaching the gospel were introduced in Nigeria. In the 1950s the Celestial Church of Christ arrived in western Nigeria from Benin. The church rapidly expands into northern Nigeria and became one of Africa's largest Aladura churches.[33]

Pentecostal and Neo-Pentecostal Churches

The study of Pentecostal Churches is regarded as the third phase in the history of Christianity in Nigeria. The existence of the churches in this category is a challenge to the existence of mainline and African Independent Churches. Some of these Churches are the Deeper Life Bible Church, the Redeemed Christian Church of God (RCCG), the Redeemed Evangelical Mission (TREM) the Latter Rain Assemblies, House of God Mission, Christ Embassy and Living Faith Church, aka Winners Chapel.

As alluded to above, the history of Indegenous Pentecostalism in Nigeria is also that of the African indegenous churches in the CAN bloc of OAIC. Around 1910, Garrick Braide, an Anglican Catechist in Niger-Delta area launched an indigenous prophetic movement and after his death, his followers became the Christ Army Church. Following an influenza epidemic in 1918, revivals flare within the mission churches.[34]

In 1918, an Anglican formed a prayer group known as the Precious Stone, later called Diamond Society to heal influenza victims.[35] The group leaves the Anglican Church in the early 1920s and affiliates with Faith Tabernacle, a church based in Philadelphia.[36] In 1930s, Joseph Babalola of Faith Tabernacle leads a revival that converts thousands. In 1932, his movement initiates ties with the Pentecostal Apostolic Church of Great Britain after coming into conflict with colonial authorities, but the association dissolves over the use of modern medicine. In 1941, Babalola founds the independent Christ Apostolic Church.[37]

During this period, the foreign Pentecostal denominations such as the Welsh Apostolic Church (1931), the Assemblies of God (1939) and the Foursquare Gospel Church (1941) and followed by Apostolic Faith (1944) were also introduced into Nigeria[38]. This period was characterized by interactions between indigenous Pentecostal forms called Aladura and these foreign denominational Pentecostal churches.

The next period in this phase of Christianity in Nigeria started in the 1960s. Nigeria had witnessed a phenomenal growth in the establishment of Pentecostal churches. Pentecostal churches have become many in number. It is argued by Chris Obi, quoting Larry Christensen that Pentecostal churches are seen as a supernatural manifestation of the Holy Spirit, whereby the believer speaks forth in a language he never learned, and which he does not understand.[39]

The churches often started as non-denominational Christian fellowship centers before they metamorphosed into churches, such as the Deeper Life Bible Church founded in 1973, and soon became one of Nigeria's largest classical Pentecostal churches. With over 500 churches in Lagos, 5,000 in the rest of Nigeria, current estimated 800,000 members in Nigeria and missionaries to 40 countries in Africa[40]with the headquarters in Lagos, under the leadership of Pastor William Kumuyi.

Earlier in 1952, a former member of the Cherubim and Seraphim society, Pa Josiah Akindayomi, founded the Redeemed Christian Church of God. He was succeeded by Pastor Enoch Adejare Adeboye in 1981.[41]The Redeemed Christian Church of God started at Willoughby Street, Ebute-Metta, Lagos with a house fellowship called, the Glory of God Fellowship. Initially there were nine members but before long the fellowship rapidly grew as the news of the miracles that occurred in their midst spread. Rev. Akindayomi also had a vision of the name of the ministry that appeared to be written on a blackboard. The words were 'The Redeemed Christian

Church of God[42]The church became increasingly Pentecostal in theology and practice and today in 2017 has grown many parishes in Nigeria and present in 180 countries of the world.[43]

Others are the Living Faith Church, aka Winners Chapel founded by Bishop David Oyedepo in 1986 with current headquarters in Ota, Ogun State, where he sited "Faith Tabernacle" in 1999 that seats 50,000 worshippers, built within a year.[44] Oyedepo is also interested in circular education, apart from his Word of Faith Bible Institute that has 60 campuses all over Africa. He is the founder of Kingdom Heritage Nursery Primary School that has its presence in virtually all the states in Nigeria. He is also the founder of the Faith Academy, a model Christian college and the Chancellor of Covenant and Landmark universities in Ota and Omu-aran respectively. His aim for these educational institutions is to embark on raising a new generation of leaders in various fields of human endeavors by a training methodology that emphasises skill and character.[45]

Other Pentecostal churches in Nigeria are the Church of God Mission, Benin-City founded by late Benson Idahosa in 1972 and now being led by his wife Bishop Margaret Idahosa, Pastor Tunde Bakare's Latter Rain Assembly in Lagos, Pastor Chris Oyakhilome of Christ Embassy Church also in Lagos. Originating in evangelical student revivals, a wave of Pentecostal expansion spawns new churches in the 1970s. New charismatic churches grew throughout the 1980s and 1990s. The period from the early 1990s till date witnessed a new era of the neo Pentecostal churches. Asaju in his view on the rise of Pentecostal churches in Nigeria posited that Pentecostalism in Nigeria initially began as a reaction to the pronounced legalism and orthodoxy of the mainline mission churches.[46] He was of the opinion that the resistance of the mainline churches of doctrines such as faith healing, exorcism, speaking in tongues, vision and prophecy, as well as charismatic expression in songs and worship[47] led to mass exodus of their members to the newly founded Pentecostal churches in Nigeria.

The neo Pentecostal move features a relaxation of the classical 'holiness doctrine'. The emphasis is now on the prosperity gospel and faith. Few of them also emphasize on deliverance and healing. Churches like Mountain of Fire and Miracle established in 1989 by Dr. D. K. Olukoya, Christ Embassy in 1991 by Pastor Chris Oyakhilome, House on the Rock in 1994 by Pastor Paul Adefarasin and Daystar Christian Centre in 1995 by

Pastor Sam Adeyemi and many more springing up daily. These churches were founded and led by young, upward mobile, educated professionals who appropriated modern marketing techniques in their evangelism.[48]

Some of the Pentecostal and neo-Pentecostal churches have taken over public space hitherto considered unconventional for worship purposes. They have also thoroughly put the mass media into their evangelism strategy. Unemployment, poverty, poor health care and hardship generally have driven many Nigerians into the Pentecostal churches that promised miracles, prosperity and 'breakthrough.'

Conclusion

The advent of Christianity in the area now called Nigeria was the beginning of many good things that were to happen. Education, civilization, national development, trade and commerce were all affected and scaled up. The mainline churches as the first comers became well established and wielded massive power and authority in all spheres of peoples' lives, community life and held sway in national life. The arrival of the Pentecostal churches from the early 20th century announced a different perspective to the faith introduced by the missionaries. The initial challenge posed by the first and second streams of Pentecostalism and later neo-Pentecostalism meant that the mainline churches in Nigeria were operating from a position of threat, concern and even, in some instances, fear about the future of their church. The impact of neo-Pentecostalism has left the mainline churches with very little room to manoeuvre. Their very survival has come to depend not on their historic achievements in education and social work, but on how open they are to a Pentecostalism. A space of competition was created in the Nigerian religious landscape. The mainline churches were influenced by the high wave of Pentecostalism and this in effect affected their traditions and idiosyncrasies. Making them Pentecostal and charismatic in order to keep their members and toning down their western trademarks, making the church relevant to an average Nigerian. However, there is a current paradigm shift. Some Pentecostal churches are now imbibing and emulating some of the traditions and practices of the mainline churches in the use of titles, vestment, liturgy and many other areas we shall investigate later.

Notes and References

1   Rotimi Omotoye, "The Concept of God and its Understanding by the Christian Missionaries in Yorubaland" in E. Ade Odumuyiwa (ed), *God: The Contemporary Discussion* (Ilorin: Decency Printers, 2005), 105.

2   Christian Association of Nigeria, *About CAN*, http://canng.org/about-can/blocs (accessed August 17, 2017 at 11.00am).

3   Rotimi Omotoye, "A Critical Examination of The Activities Of Pentecostal Churches In National Development In Nigeria" *Centre for Studies Of New Religions – The Journal of Cesnur.* http://www.cesnur. org/2010/omotoye.htm(accessed August 17, 2017 at 11.00am).

4   Ogbu Kalu, *Christianity in West Africa, the Nigerian Story*, (Ibadan: Daystar press, 1978), 255.

5   Adepeju O. Bashua, CRS 827: Missiology, 2017, 30.

6   Bashua, 30.

7   Omotoye, 105.

8   Bashua, 30.

9   Joseph Kehinde Adekanye, *The Church of God – History, Doctrine & Liturgy (The Anglican Perspective)*, (Lagos: Paraclete, 2015), 291.

10 The Vanguard, "News", https://www.vanguardngr.com/2012/10/methodist-church-nigeria-170-years-ofimpacting-nigeria-for-god/ (accessed August 25, 2017 at 7.00pm).

11 The Vanguard, "News" (accessed August 25, 2017).

12 The Vanguard, "News" (accessed August 25, 2017).

13 World Council of Churches, Members, https://www.oikoumene.org/en/member-churches/methodist-church-nigeria (accessed August 25, 2017 at 7.50pm).

14 See http://immanuelcollege.edu.ng and Joseph Kehinde Adekanye, *The Church of God – History, Doctrine & Liturgy (The Anglican Perspective)*, (Lagos: Paraclete, 2015), 315.

15 Bashua, 30.

16 Adekanye, 291.

17 Bashua, 34-52.

18 Michael, Olusina Fape, *Knowing the Fundamentals of Anglicanism* (Sagamu: Joas Press, 2010), Fape, 65-67.

[19] Fape, v.

[20] Adeniyi, Edward Adebayo, *Elements of Anglicanism*, (Akure: Bosem Publishers Ltd, 2012), 73-85.

[21] Church of Nigeria, About us, https://anglican-nig.org/about-us/ (accessed 24th June, 2017).

[22] Fape, 64.

[23] Fape, 65-67.

[24] Bashua, 63-73.

[25] Samuel Adetunji Fatokun, "The Distinctive Features of Aladura Movement and their Implication for African Pentecostalism" *SPECTRUM Journal of Contemporary Christianity and Society*, Vol. 2, No 1 (2017): 30-31.

[26] Fatokun, "The Distinctive…, 30-33.

[27] Fatokun, "The Distinctive…., 30.

[28] Fatokun, "The Distinctive…, 30.

[29] Deji Ayegboyin, "Resonance of African Initiated Churches' Beliefs and Practices in Nigerian Pentecostal Praxis," *SPECTRUM Journal of Contemporary Christianity and Society*, Vol. 2, No 1 (2017): 5-6.

[30] Fatokun, "The Distinctive…, 30.

[31] Akin Omoyajowo, "The Aladura Churches in Nigeria since Independence" Edward Fashole-Luke (ed) et al *Christianity in Independent Africa*, London: Rex Collins, 1979, 96.

[32] Rotimi Omotoye, "Christianity and Cultural Development: An Examination of Aladura churches in Yorubaland" in Ade P. Dopamu (ed), *Dialogue issues in contemporary Discussion*, (Lagos, Big Small, 2007), 335-340.

[33] Rotimi Omotoye "A Critical Examination… (accessed August 17, 2017 at 11.00am).

[34] Ayodeji Abodunde, *Messenger: Sydney Elton and the Making of Pentecostalism in Nigeria*, (Lagos: Pierce Watershed, 2016), 26.

[35] Abodunde, 29.

[36] Abodunde, 29.

[37] Dairo Afolorunso Olalekan, "…Being in the World and not Part of the World" The Changing Faces of Pentecostalism in the 21st Century Nigeria" *SPECTRUM Journal of Contemporary Christianity and Society*, Vol. 2, No 1 (2017): 52.

[38] Olalekan, 51.

[39] Rotimi Omotoye, "Communication and the Universality of the Gospel in Yorubaland" in Ade P. Dopamu (ed), *Science and Religion in the service of Humanity*, (Ilorin, Local Society Initiatives LSI, 2006), 42.

[40] Deeper Christian Life Ministry, Pastor W. F. Kumuyi, http://dclm.org/about/pastor-w-f-kumuyi/ (accessed August 24, 2017 at 2.50pm).

[41] The Redeemed Christian Church of God, Who we are, http://rccg.org/who-we-are/history/ (accessed August 17, 2017 at 3.00pm).

[42] The Redeemed Christian Church of God, Who we are, (accessed August 17, 2017 at 7.50pm).

[43] The Redeemed Christian Church of God, Who we are, (accessed August 17, 2017 at 7.50pm).

[44] Deji Ayegboyin, "New Pentecostal Churches and Prosperity Theology in Nigeria" in Afe Adogame (ed), *Who is Afraid of the Holy Ghost? Pentecostalism and Globalization in Africa and Beyond*, (New Jersey: Africa World Press, 2011), 164.

[45] Faith Tabernacle, Education, http://faithtabernacle.org.ng/education/ (accessed August 17, 2017 at 7.50pm).

[46] Dapo F. Asaju, "Globalization, Politicization of Religion and Religious Networking – The Case of the Pentecostal Fellowship of Nigeria" in Afe Adogame (ed), *Who is Afraid of the Holy Ghost? Pentecostalism and Globalization in Africa and Beyond*, (New Jersey: Africa World Press, 2011), 188.

[47] Dapo F. Asaju, "Globalization…, 188-189.

[48] Titilayo Falola, *The History of Nigeria* (Westport: Greenwood Press, 1999), 183-204.

CHAPTER THREE

INFLUENCE OF PENTECOSTALISM ON MAINLINE CHURCHES: THE MISSION

✠   ✠   ✠

Pentecostalism since inception has enormously influenced the mainline churches. We are set to analyse areas of these influences which we present as mission to the mainline churches. Many people believe that the impact of Pentecostalism in Nigeria cannot be overlooked, especially on the mainline churches. We are poised to identify areas of direct and indirect influences.

Prayer and Spirituality

The mainline churches have their traditional, often stereotyped style of praying. For example, the Anglican prayer identity is the Book of Common Prayer (BCP). The Anglican Communion was traditionally bound together among other things by the BCP of the Church of England. Deacons, priests as well as bishops at ordination and consecration are made to take oath by using the BCP. The BCP contains all manners of intercessory prayers. These prayers are referred to as Collects.[1] There are Collects for every season throughout the year, for special needs and different occasions. They are said or sung in all Anglican regular and occasional services. However,

Pentecostalism is well known for its prayer dynamism with extempore prayers believed to be inspired by the Holy Spirit. The Pentecostals have gained prominence due to their aggressive evangelistic campaigns[2] including the use of deliverance prayers, prophetic declarations and words of knowledge. There is much emphasis on matters such as the 'praying in the Spirit', 'baptism of the Spirit', 'being filled with the Spirit' and 'walking in the Spirit'.[3] Ogbu had rightly observed how these Pentecostal dynamism and features have drastically reshaped the face of African Christianity.[4]

It has been observed that an average Nigerian is no longer comfortable with only Collects read or sung from the BCP, some composed in 1662 or earlier. The average Nigerian wants prayer that will touch his life directly and for him to say a loud Amen. Due to the influence of Pentecostalism, extempore prayers are now richly led by the conductor after reading or singing the collects. Service leaders and Anglican clerics have had to learn the art of praying extemporaneously. Many mainline churches have today employed a wholesale adoption of Pentecostal prayer dynamics to make the Christian faith more relevant to their members. The fact that the Western worldview is different from the African milieu is a reality today. There is no doubt that Pentecostalism has awakened in mainline churches' members an eagerness for spiritual life in the secular world, and a desire for an experiential communion with God in prayers. Prayer schools, healing schools, healing bay, prayer chain, faith clinics, prayer walk and prayer line are some Pentecostal prayer idiosyncrasies.[5] These are today finding their ways into the mainline churches.

Special Spiritual Programmes

Initially, virtually all the mainline churches were satisfied with their statutory services on Sunday morning and evening. Occasional services like funeral, wedding and anniversary are statutory and sacerdotal work of the clergy. But today, due to the influence of Pentecostalism, many mainline churches now conduct crusades and open-air revival services. Numerous other spiritual programmes are now being organised for members' spiritual growth and expression of faith. Like the annual popular Holy Ghost Convention of the Redeemed Christian Church of God and Shiloh of the Living Faith Church, virtually all mainline churches in Nigeria have such annual conventions to pull their members together, to ensure they do not leave for other churches. For example in the Anglican Church; the Primate of All Nigeria, the Most Revd Nicholas Okoh started an annual highly spiritual one week evangelical crusade and conference tagged *Divine Commonwealth Conference* (DIVCCON) in Abuja which holds every November.[6] It is usually a gathering of charismatic and evangelical Anglican members from across the world to participate in prayers, crusade, revival, seminar and Bible study under God for blessings, miracles, signs and wonders. Testimonies of divine intervention are shared annually.

It is also noticed that camp grounds are being bought by many mainline churches, like the Pentecostal churches.[7] Many Pentecostal churches are noted by the culture of inculcating a spirituality which is communitarian, by establishing 'holy cities' and camps to which they converge from across the world at least once in a year.[8] Like Canaanland of the Living Faith Church, Redemption Camp of the Redeemed Christian Church of God and the Prayer City of the Mountain of Fire and Miracle ministries.

Vigil

There was nothing like vigil in the contemporary style in mainline churches at inception in Nigeria. Except some liturgical ones, like in the traditional Anglican forms; vigils were held twice in a year, the Easter and New Year's Eve vigils. But today, due to the influence of Pentecostalism, many mainline churches now hold vigils monthly and quarterly. Radio and television adverts are often heard and seen; posters are often viewed in public places inviting members of the public to attend. Such are mainly attended by children, youths and charismatic members of the church. It is widely believed that attending vigils has enhanced the spiritual lives of such members. Testimonies are often well publicised.

Preaching God's word

Some outstanding Pentecostal pastors are revered for the passion with which they teach and preach the good news, Christian faith and morals.

For example, Pastor Williams Kumuyi of the Deeper Life Bible Church is widely known for his down to earth Biblical interpretation and application. Such has motivated preachers and clergy of the mainline churches to give a new zeal to the ministry of the Word. Lay and charismatic members in many mainline churches are now being encouraged to take courses in Bible schools in order to serve as evangelists to spread the Gospel. This desire for a renew commitment to the preaching and teaching of the Christian faith is a contribution of Pentecostalism. It is observed that the initial lethargic preachers in some mainline churches are now being challenged by Pentecostals to brace up, and the pulpits in the mainline churches are becoming fountain of enrichment and nourishment for the members. It is now widely observed that clergy of the mainline churches have not only adjusted to this form of preaching but now, boldly organize crusades, revival services and preach in similar level of effective communication of God's word.

Liturgy – Worship

Ayegboyin argued that Pentecostalism was a revolt against the formal and almost monotonous liturgy in the historic churches.[9] The mission churches at inception were guilty of not giving room for local theology in which the seed of faith is allowed to interact with the native soil, leading to a new flowering of Christianity, faithful both to the local culture and to the apostolic faith.[10] The missionaries did not allow natives to beat drums and clap their hands in the African vivacious nature. It is not simply that early Anglican missionaries assumed that their British values and approaches were intrinsically correct; they also ignored or suppressed the cultural and social roots of those whom they ministered.[11] For example, the missionaries were against any form of African tradition, cultural norms and heritage. The language and native music were repulsive to them.

The liturgy of the Anglican Church was crafted by Archbishop Thomas Crammer, who also wrote the BCP. It is stereotyped and arranged from Advent[12] to Trinity.[13] The Psalms and scriptural readings are already arranged in the lectionary for services and occasions. Therefore, an average Anglican or Methodist priest is rest assured that all is set for the whole year. Whereas, it is widely noted that the Pentecostals do not have such lectionaries and written liturgy. When some of Pentecostal churches even have an order of service, it could be changed now and again provided to them, it is in harmony with the 'leading of the Holy Spirit'. The Pentecostal form of worship was not encumbered with formalities, creedal statements and stereotypical outlines.[14]

The Pentecostals' attention to worship and vibrancy of Pentecostal celebrations have led to a change of attitude towards liturgical celebrations in the mainline churches. Today, a liberal position is being maintained by most mainline churches and that as good as the liturgy is, the clergy is free to control it and not the other way round. Dynamism, contextualisation and initiative are now being brought it to allow the Holy Spirit to move. It is believed that rigidity to the liturgy and lectionaries most often distant the Holy Spirit from such liturgical services. But flexibility at times gives room for service leaders to hear from the Holy Spirit. The guiding principles for preparing for any liturgical function, is built around the experience of the people and not simply in conformity to a foreign style of worship. Many Nigerians Christians generally welcome the Pentecostal style of worship, since this seems to respond to African religious sentiments. Harley and Sybertz opined that:

> It is now taken for granted that some of these basic anthropological dispositions of Africans could become useful and powerful tools for glorifying God and edifying a worshiping community.[15]

In some mainline churches today, like the Anglican Church, certain Sundays in the month are now being used for revival and youth services that are non-liturgical. Many mainline churches now conduct miracle and healing, deliverance and anointing services.

Participation of Members in Worship and Church Life

The advent of Christianity and its growth in the mainline churches had the clergy at the centre of everything in the church. He was the teacher, the head teacher, the government representative, and carried out many other responsibilities. But due to the influence of Pentecostalism, there is a kind of division of labour. Even the Holy Communion service in the Anglican Church, which is the highest liturgical service, could be conducted in part by lay members, like, the Ante-Communion,[16]which is the first part of the service. Lay members are now allowed to play vital roles during services and in church life, irrespective of their status. The notion is that no group in the church has monopoly of the spiritual gifts not even the priests. This is in line with Ephesians 4:11-14, that the body of Christ grows and benefits where there are manifestations of spiritual gifts, either among the laity or the clergy. Members of the mainline churches are now allowed to lead different departments where their gifts could be used to benefit the body of Christ, ordained or not.

Roles of Women in Church Ministry

Bateye aptly posited that the colonial churches (mainline churches) were expatriate administered bodies that reflected the gender biases of the colonial masters that discriminated against women.[17] It was also pertinent that black male preachers were also discriminated against at that time. The mainline missionaries believed then that black men and especially women were not qualified to lead a church. This partly led some blacks to secede and form their own independent churches. But lately, due to the influence of Pentecostal churches, women in the mainline churches, who until recently played a passive and supportive role are now allowed to participate effectively in church life. The era when the church was the exclusive affairs of the male clergy is fast coming to an end. The Pentecostal consciousness where women are church founders and are ordained pastors and the Biblical concept of priesthood of all believers have really encouraged many mainline churches to have a rethink about women ordination. For example, in the Anglican Church, the church in the West and other parts of Africa has since been ordaining female clergy. Some members of the Anglican Church of Nigeria are strongly pushing for women ordination currently.

Oyalana aptly suggests that the question of women ordination to the priesthood of the church is an explosive matter.[18] Imasuen and Atowoju refer to the repudiation of the ordination of women carried out by the retired Bishop of the Anglican Diocese of Kwara some years ago.[19] In 2013 at the church's General Synod[20] at Enugu, the General Synod overwhelmingly voted against the proposal for ordination of women in the Nigerian Anglican Church. Of the 514 participants in the Synod, 482 voted against while 32 voted for, the women who participated voted with 211 against two.[21] However, there are ongoing consultations and theological debates to ensure that majority support the move. In other words, the agenda is always presented at all such meetings of the Anglican Church in Nigeria. Some mainline churches now give conspicuous places for women today due to the influence of Pentecostal churches. Mainline churches strictly restricting the roles of women in their leadership as a result of Paul's injunction about women in 1Corinthians 14:34-35, and some social and cultural limitations are being influenced to revisit that position.

Ministerial Formation and Training of Lay Members

Due to the influence of Pentecostalism, many mainline churches now have Bible colleges. This is different from the seminary where clergy are trained before ordination. Virtually all dioceses in Lagos Province of the Anglican Church have Bible colleges. The aim is to create a forum of learning for lay people who are interested in the study of the Bible and its advanced related disciplines in the fields of Theology.[22]

Lay members are sent there for training in church doctrines, ministry and other theological foundational courses to enable them function well in their lay ministerial call.

The influence of Pentecostalism has also facilitated mainline seminaries to review the programmes of formation of their priests, in order to respond effectively, to the 21st century situation in the country. For example, the Anglican Theological Seminaries in Nigeria recently reviewed their curriculum to attend to the needs of the time. The European imported programme of formation has been reviewed and contextualised. For example the reviewed vision of Archbishop Vining College of Theology Akure, Ondo State; a frontline Anglican seminary in Nigeria is developing a college of international status, to deliver relevant and effective, contextual, spiritual and academic training of clergy and laity to meet 21st century challenges, in a friendly and healthy environment.[23] And apart from the ministerial training in the seminaries and theological faculties, the mainline churches' clerics are further exposed to various denominational and interdenominational centres for training and retraining. The aim is to enable them to minister properly to the contemporary Christians.

Media and Communication

Another aspect of this response is the development of communication departments in the mainline churches. For instance, the Anglican Church's bishops and priests are now regular guests in television and radio stations, in their attempt to carry the gospel beyond the pulpit. There is a weekly 30 minutes sermon aired in Muhri International Television (MITV), Ikeja, Lagos from 3 - 3.30pm every Sunday. Hess, while harping on the importance of media to religious institutions, opines that the experience of feeling connected to people beyond one's immediate context, and to experience beyond one's imagining, occurs more often through mass media technologies than it does in any other way.[24] Church programmes and spiritual activities are given wider publicity in the mass media. The Pentecostals have encouraged the use of mass media for religious programmes, and this is fast rubbing off on many mainline churches. An example of this is that in the year 2013 the Church of Nigeria, Anglican Communion launched its cable network; Anglican Cable Network Nigeria (ACNN), Channel 91 in MyTV. It is her window into the world to disseminate the Gospel of Christ to the world. In the words of Hess, the Anglican Church now has

> courtesy of media technologies, compelling representations of life lived in multiple faiths, many of which are far distant from Christianity. They now have, courtesy of media technologies, multiple ways in which to capture their imagination and cede their territories to all kinds of dreams.[25]

In other words, the church is no longer localized, but globalized. The times of traditional withdrawal of mainline churches into enclaves of faith are past. Many today are out to contest public space in the media. Such development was engendered by the influence of Pentecostalism.

Church Consciousness

Pentecostalism has really influenced church affinity and consciousness of many Christians. Today, many members of mainline churches freely and joyfully identify with their churches and dioceses. The personal feeling of being part of an organised Body of Christ is usually exciting today. It is now very common to see members of a particular mainline church or diocese proudly wearing wrist-bands and pasting on their door-posts and vehicles stickers of their church or diocese. It is not contestable that the Pentecostals introduced such consciousness and church solidarity. Such denominational identities were really non-existent many years back.

Tithes and Offerings

For instance, in the Western mission churches, like the Anglican Church at inception, foreign aids and grants from bodies and agencies in the 'mother' Church of England were available. There also used to be payment of 'class fee'. More so, rights and privileges were usually attached to this annual levy. No one could occupy any position in the church if defaulting, and no funeral service for such a person would be conducted until all outstanding class fees were settled by the deceased's family. This, with the annual harvest due, Easter and New Year dues is the expected financial commitments of each member.[26] The proceeds of these put together are used for church maintenance, payment of assessment levy to the diocese from where the priest draws his salary and developmental projects.

However, the Pentecostal churches, except for few who have affiliate bodies that support them, are often indigenous congregations and as such look inward for their financing and sustenance. They teach, encourage and monitor their members to pay promptly and faithfully their tithes, which they generally accepted. The practice has been very successful in Nigeria. Many mainline churches are amazed and intrigued by the success to raise funds through tithing and execute large projects. Overtime, the mainline churches began to realise the 'spiritual usefulness' of tithing, and therefore introduced tithing to support their churches. For example, priests across the Anglican Church in Nigeria now teach their members through Bible study and preaching to pay tithe. The influence of Pentecostalism in this regard is very clear, as many Anglicans today pay their tithes, which generate more funds to the church, than the 'class fee' and other levies. For example, Odukoya while enumerating the Anglican parish income opined that tithes are the major church's income.[27]

Spirituality and Devotional Life

One of the religious experiences in Pentecostalism that has come to stay in the mainline churches today is speaking in tongues: 'glossolalia'. Even though some mainline churches do not yet allow speaking in tongues in their public liturgy, they still term it as disruptive, breaking down decorum and order.[28] Paul's advice to the Corinthian church (1Corinthians 14:27-28) that tongues must be interpreted or such speaker should keep quiet also enhanced their argument against speaking in tongues publicly. Still, it is becoming a common phenomenon in revival and prayer services in the most mainline churches for members to speak in tongues, even when there is no interpreter. There are mainline bishops, priests and ministers who now openly speak in tongues and encourage their members to pray in tongues.[29] Some manifestations associated with the experience of the Holy Spirit are now common in some mainline churches both at public and private levels.

Another Pentecostal practice that is incorporated by many mainline churches is voluptuous praise. Priests and pastors now urge members to praise the Lord, and dance before the Lord. For example, the Anglican liturgy now accommodates praise and worship at the beginning of the divine and even Holy Communion services.[30]

It is widely accepted that Pentecostalism is a blessing to the contemporary mainline churches. It has created visible and enduring impact on their identities and practices. In other words, the revival of Pentecostalism is no longer a blessing to the Pentecostal churches alone, but the mainline churches. Many are now very comfortable to stay in their old churches due to the high spirituality and ample opportunity to grow their faith into maturity and the assurance of making heaven at last.

University Education

Mainline churches no doubt opened up Nigeria to western education with the mission schools administered by the missionaries and later by the clergy. These were however forcefully taken over by the government in the 1970s.[31] But the Pentecostal churches were first to break the grounds in university education. For example, the Church of God Mission's Benson Idahosa University, Benin city in 2002, the Living Faith Church's Covenant University, Ota in 2002 and later in 2011 Landmark University, Omu-aran and the Redeemer's University, Ede of the Redeemed Christian Church of God in 2005[32] are world-class Universities. Although according to Asaju:

> These private universities are run as commercial-profit oriented ventures, not as mission institutions, their fees are far beyond the reach of middle class citizens, nor even affordable by majority of the church members whose monies were used to set up such institutions.[33]

It is however believed by many that the above Pentecostal churches and many others have contributed immensely to national development and have complemented the efforts of the government in the provision of western education, manpower, employment and civilization in Nigeria. Such motivation and financial benefits have influenced the mainline churches to also launch their private universities. For example, Ajayi Crowther University, Oyo of the Supra-West Anglican Church founded in 2005, Wesley University of Science and Technology, Ondo of the Methodist Church, Nigeria in 2007.[34]

Conclusion

We submit that Pentecostalism no doubt has thoroughly influenced other existing mainline churches. It has been effective in bringing people into a personal relationship with God through Jesus Christ, in the power of the Holy Spirit. It encourages its members to share their personal spiritual experience and testimonies with others, to live holy lives according to the Bible, to embrace good works as part of the Spirit-filled life and fruit of the Spirit, to be open to the sovereign movement of the Holy Spirit through gifts, signs and wonders, and to support the work of the church through their offerings, seed sowing and regular tithing. It is widely accepted that this Pentecostal spirit is moving across all denominations. We cannot ignore the fact that Pentecostal churches are source of inspiration to many Nigerians and they are really making a great impact in the spread of the Gospel.

Notes and References

1   Collect is a short general <u>prayer</u> of a particular structure used in <u>Christian liturgy</u>.

2   Philomena Njeri Mwaura, "The Role of Charismatic Christianity in Reshaping the Religious Scene in Africa: The Case of Kenya" in Afe Adogame, Roswith Gerloff & Klaus Hock (eds), *Christianity in Africa and the African Diaspora* (London, New York: Continuum, 2008), 180.

3   Deji Ayegboyin, "Resonance of African Initiated Churches' Beliefs and Practices in Nigerian Pentecostal Praxis" *SPECTRUM Journal of Contemporary Christianity and Society*, Vol. 2, No 1 (2017): 10.

4   Kalu Ogbu, *Power, Poverty and Prayer: The Challenge of Poverty and Pluralism in African Christianity 1960-1996* (Frankfurt: Peter Lang, 2000), 103.

5   Asaju, Dapo, Keynote address on *African Pentecostalism and development in Africa and Diaspora* at International Conference of African Pentecostalism (ICAP 2017), at The Redeemed Christian Bible College, Mowe, Nigeria 13-15 June 2017.

6   Divine Commonwealth Conference, "About", http://www.divccon2017.org/ (accessed on 05/10/2017 @ 2.40pm).

7   Ayegboyin, "Resonance of African...", 24-25.

8   Ayegboyin, "Resonance of African...", 24-25.

9   Ayegboyin, "Resonance of African Initiated Churches' Beliefs and Practices in Nigerian Pentecostal Praxis" *SPECTRUM Journal of Contemporary Christianity and Society*, Vol. 2, No 1 (2017): 19.

10 Robert J. Schreiter, *Constructing Local Theologies*, (New York: Orbis, 1986), 11.

11 Alister E. McGrath, *The Renewal of Anglicanism*, (London: SPCK, 1993), 22.

12 Advent is a season observed in many Christian churches as a time of expectant waiting and preparation for the celebration of the Nativity of Jesus at Christmas. The term is a version of the Latin word meaning "coming".

13 Trinity Sunday is the first Sunday after Pentecost in the Western Christian liturgical calendar

14 Deji Ayegboyin, "Resonance...", 19-20.

[15] Joseph Healey and Donald Sybertz, *Towards an African Narrative Theology*, (Nairobi: Paulines Publications Africa, 1996), 260-261.

[16] Ante-Communion is earlier part of the Communion service in the Book of Common Prayer, which extends from the beginning of the office to the end of the general prayer

[17] Bolaji Bateye, "Female Religious Leadership in Nigeria Pentecostalism: Embers or Gale?" in Afe Adogame (ed), *Who is Afraid of the Holy Ghost? Pentecostalism and Globalization in Africa and Beyond*, New Jersey: Africa World Press, 2011), 38-39.

[18] A. S. Oyalana, Christian Witnessing in Nigeria, (Ibadan: Daystar Press, 2005), 70.

[19] Peter O. J. Imasuen and Ayodele A. Atowoju, Christian Worship & Pastoral Ministry, (Ibadan: Daystar Press, 2008), 121.

[20] General Synod is the highest decision body of the church and holds every three years with delegates of eight members nominated from each diocese of the Church in Nigeria

[21] The Vanguard, "News", http://www.vanguardngr.com/2014/12/anglicans-vote-ordination-women/ (retrieved 03/08/2017 at 5am).

[22] Diocese of Remo, "Schools", http://remoanglican.org/schools/diocesan-school-of-theology/ (retrieved 04/08/2017 at 7.45am).

[23] Vining College, *"Mission and Vision"*, http://viningcollegeakure.org/visionmission/ (retrieved 04/08/2017 at 8.45am).

[24] Mary E. Hess, "Practising Attention in Media Culture" in Jolyon Mitchell & Sophia Marriage (eds), *Mediating Religion – Conversation in Media, Religion and Culture* (London, New York: T & T Clark Ltd, 2006), 138.

[25] Hess, 142.

[26] The Church of Nigeria (Anglican Communion), *Constitution of the Diocesan Synod*, Diocese of Awori, (Chapter XI, Section 3b, 2008), 31.

[27] Bayo, Odukoya "Church Management and Administration" a paper presented at the All Anglican Clergy Conference @ the University of Nigeria Nsukka, 2008, 228.

[28] Ogbu U. Kalu, "Who is Afraid of the Holy Ghost? Presbyterians and Early Charismatic Movement in Nigeria, 1966-1975" in Afe Adogame (ed), *Who is Afraid of the Holy Ghost? Pentecostalism and Globalization in Africa and Beyond*, New Jersey: Africa World Press, 2011), 106.

29 Dapo Asaju, Keynote address on *African Pentecostalism and development in Africa and Dispora* at International Conference of African Pentecostalism (ICAP 2017), at The Redeemed Christian Bible College, Mowe, Nigeria 13-15 June 2017.

30 Edmund, Akanya "Anglican Liturgy and Challenges of Pentecostalism/ Charismatism" a paper presented at the All Anglican Clergy Conference @ the University of Nigeria Nsukka, 2008, 57-65.

31 Education in Nigeria, http://www.onlinenigeria.com/education/ (accessed on 05/10/2017 @ 5.00pm).

32 National Universities Commission, Private Universities, http://nuc.edu. ng/nigerian-univerisities/private-univeristies/(accessed on 05/10/2017 @ 5.00pm).

33 Dapo F. Asaju, "Globalization, Politicization of Religious Network – The Case of the Pentecostal Fellowship of Nigeria" in Afe Adogame (ed), *Who is Afraid of the Holy Ghost? Pentecostalism and Globalization in Africa and Beyond*, New Jersey: Africa World Press, 2011), 193.

34 National Universities Commission, Private Universities, http://nuc.edu. ng/nigerian-univerisities/private-univeristies/(accessed on 05/10/2017 @ 5.00pm).

CHAPTER FOUR

INFLUENCE OF MAINLINE CHURCHES ON PENTECOSTAL CHURCHES: A REVERSE MISSION

✠   ✠   ✠

Asaju, while arguing in favour of the influence of mainline churches on Pentecostal churches queried the identity of the Pentecostals when many Pentecostals have radically returned to the vestments, the liturgies and the traditions of the mainline churches which they hitherto criticized.[1]It became obvious lately that some Pentecostal churches that initially criticised many perceived wrongs are fast picking up some of the primordial and Victorian legacies of some mainline churches' identities. Pentecostal leaders who initially were believed to have condemned and demonised virtually everything about the mainline churches' traditions and practices, are now appreciating some of these Biblical and cultural identities, they now realise that such are not necessarily inimical to the Christian faith. We shall highlight some of the current paradigm shifts of the Pentecostal churches in imbibing some of the traditions and practices.

As earlier stated, we are using the technical concept of reverse mission to bring such practices and traditions to limelight. Reverse mission as far as our work is concerned is the current influence of the mainline churches on the Pentecostal churches that earlier had wielded a strong and massive influence at inception. Areas of initial Pentecostal churches' repulsion and outright rejection now become part of their new practices. Some have been repackaged and adopted, some taken hook, line and sinker. We have attempted to establish that the influences are not one sided, but bipartite.

Scholarship has recently noted the reversal of the initial massive influence of Pentecostalism on the mainline churches[2]. Reverse mission therefore, is the reverse phenomenon of the initial influence of Pentecostal churches. In other words, noticeable reverse waves have caught our observation on the influence of the mainline churches on classical and neo-Pentecostal churches. The following are identified:

Liturgy and Procession

'Liturgy' comes from Greek, the language used by the early church in its worship and writings. It derives from the word *leitourgia* which referred to any public service or function exercised by the people as a whole. By its nature, liturgy is ordered worship.[3] A working definition of liturgy that is helpful is the official and public worship of the church. While worship can be a private act, liturgy is always a communal activity.[4] Liturgy celebrates the mystery that is God. This is the fundamental truth on which the celebration of all the church's rite depends. Over the years the mainline churches developed their liturgy. Although the New Testament does not instruct worshippers on a specific format to follow in their services, several elements appear regularly in the worship practices of the early church.[5] Mainline churches' liturgy comprises:

> Prayer (1Thessalonians 5:17), praise and hymns (Matthew 26:30, Colossian 3:16), Reading scriptural passages which originated from the Jewish temple worship (Luke 4:16-20), prophecy and preaching which was very common in Jesus ministry and offerings (1Corinthians 16:2).[6]

The essence and importance of liturgy as an official order of worship is that it becomes an element in the life of the church, as it was *Didache* i.e. the apostolic proclamation.[7] Recognition of the corporate character of worship explains the connection between the liturgy and church order. The conduct of worship cannot be left wholly to the arbitrary will of the conductor or minister. An order is needed at least to some extent fixed for uniformity in the worship life of the church. The congregation is liberated from total dependence on the clergy, his mood and limitations.[8]

Many Pentecostal churches now have a formalized order of worship as against the initial extemporaneous and spontaneous liturgy. They have arrived at a stage of re doing what they do each Sunday. This became more evident in our participant observer's worship for consecutive weeks (four services in a Sunday) at the headquarters of the Living Faith Church, Ota and a parish of the Redeemed Christian Church of God in Ota. We observed a formalized form of worship[9]. This was part of the criticism of mainline churches.

Closely following this, is Pentecostal style of singing choruses as against the mainline churches' usage of chants,[10] canticles[11] and church medieval hymns. These are used in their services and processions. What we discovered is that many Pentecostal churches now use church hymns (both contemporary and medieval) contrary to their initial choice of choruses. Some Pentecostal churches now process in and out of divine services, which until recently was an identity of mainline churches. This heritage has also been adopted by some Pentecostal churches. A procession is a royal entry and a recession an exit, not necessarily limited to a physically-present person: the Ark of the Covenant was a focus (as representative of God) of processions in the Old Testament. In worship, the cross is lifted high and always leads an opening procession and closing recession in order to laud Jesus Christ as King. The researcher during his work saw this at a prominent Pentecostal church in Ota; Rhema Christian Church and Tower as shown in the picture below.

Today the Christ Apostolic Church uses CAC Gospel Hymn book, the Apostolic Church; TAC Hymns, the Redeemed Christian Church of God uses the Redeemed Hymnal. Many believed that the Anglican hymns are biblically balanced and has been tested for many years to be valid Christian experience. Fape, while commenting on Anglican liturgy submitted that the centrality of scripture is the hallmark of Anglicanism.[12] He further argued that the Anglican liturgy as spelt out in the Book of Common Prayer[13] is the dramatization of scripture; and regardless of many editions and adaptations to the various local needs, it has a unique place in giving authentic identity to Anglicanism.[14] It is now evident that some Pentecostal churches now use such liturgy, or adapted ones in occasional services such as weddings and funerals. The researcher attended wedding ceremonies in Redeemed Christian Church of God (RCCG) and Living Faith Church parishes where similar liturgy to the mainline churches were used.[15] The only difference was that unlike in the mainline churches, where the liturgy is made open and printed along the wedding programme, the Pentecostal churches' presiding pastors alone read from their books.

The Clergy Vestments

The clerical wears and vestment were big issues of criticism at the inception of Pentecostalism in Nigeria. The clergy vestments were thoroughly condemned and messed up by some Pentecostals. It must be mentioned that the Old Testament from where church vestments originated has a vivid description of how the high priest and priests were dressed right from the time of Aaron and his sons (Exodus 28). This was however strictly followed as a rule in the old dispensation. But the early New Testament church had no special dresses or vestments for the clergy. According to Fortescue, there is no hint of special dress for clergy in the first century.[16] What later became vestments in the church were originally the common dress of both the clergy and the laity.[17] Davies explained that church vestments could be grouped into four types;

> The types worn for cultus, i.e. at the Eucharist and the
> other sacramental ceremonies, vesture for other liturgical
> occasions, some indicate ranks or specific roles and some
> are garments for customary clerical dress i.e. civilian dress
> of the clergy.[18]

He further explained that the above types came from different parts of the church; the Eastern Orthodox Church and the Roman Catholic Church.[19] But it should be noted that vestments are a development of ordinary dress. Until the 5th century A.D there was an identity of clothes between the clergy and the laity, except that the clergy put on Pallium[20] which was a badge of office. This was special scarf required by civil law to be worn by all civil officials. The clergy became civil officers in the post Constantine period.[21]

Vestments are important to the mainline churches because they communicate the nature of the occasion, show the rank of each participant and their functions.[22] Arulefela on the importance of vestments concluded that the church as the true bride of Christ has really imitated the Bridegroom who borrowed many things for the fulfilment of His ministry. What now become the vestments of the church were borrowed from the secular world she lives in.[23]

Today, many Pentecostal pastors and founders wear the same vestments they derided in the past. They even wear high churchmanship vestments, like copes and mitres. Some are now beginning to wear, clerical shirts, cassocks[24] and collars. With the obvious wrong usage of some of the vestments, it is widely observed that some Pentecostal who use them do not know the theological significance and the appropriate season and occasion for its usage.

Use of Titles

Titles of leaders of mainline churches were criticized, condemned and disdained by Pentecostals in Nigeria at inception. But today, it is observed that many Pentecostal church leaders have adopted Episcopal leadership, titles and paraphernalia. Abodunde opined that the Nigerian Pentecostal foray into mainline churches' structures and traditions broke out in November 1981 when Benson Idahosa made a surprise move, as he stood for ordination in Benin City as bishop of the Church of God Mission.[25] Idahosa was consecrated as both bishop and archbishop at the ceremony.[26] It became shocking to Pentecostals in Nigeria because they have concluded doctrinally that an ecclesiastical bishopric was antithetical to the spirit of the Pentecostal movement.[27] They never expected such Pentecostal stalwart to submit to ordination as bishop. Idahosa, who himself earlier had delighted in poking fun at ecclesiastical titles, and in his inimitable way few years earlier, he jokingly called archbishops "ashbishop" emphasizing the spiritual deadness, as he saw it, of ecclesiastical titles and structures.[28] The trend started gradually and today many Pentecostal pastors are now Reverends, Bishops and Archbishops. For example, Chris Okotie uses both the title Reverend and Pastor. Bishop Mike Okonkwo of the Redeemed Evangelical Mission (TREM), Bishop David Oyedepo of the Living Faith Church, Bishop Taiwo Akinola of the Rhema Church and Towers to mention a few.

Aesthetic and Church Building

Many mainline churches, like the Anglicans were known for Western style gothic churches and cathedrals. Even in the remotest villages and rustic locations, the church buildings usually stand out. The building committee usually saw it as *sine qua non* to copy the mother church's style of beautiful, aesthetic and architectural design with beautiful interior and adornment. The Pentecostals today also have developed a very high sense of aesthetic and beautiful interior decorations. Even those that originated from the traditionally Keswickan and Wesleyan holiness and ascetic movements now build beautiful church structures.

Administrative Set-up and Hierarchy

Some of the mainline churches are episcopally administered. For example, the structure of the Anglican Church is clearly expressed in this maxim; the Anglican Church is episcopally led and synodically governed.[30] This means that the Bishop is the spiritual and administrative head of the Diocese.[31] Their main hierarchies of church functionaries are the Bishop, Priest and the Deacon. The details and definitions of rights and responsibilities of these positions are well stated in the constitution of each mainline church. Such usually conform to the general international structure and constitutions of their parent bodies. Each person operates within his constitutional roles. Issues of discipline or breach of constitution are well handled by seasoned legal officers appointed to serve at the ecclesiastical court,[32] also referred to as Bishop's court. The synod or conference as the case may be in each mainline church is like the annual general meeting of a company. It is held once in a year with delegates of the constituent churches.[33] Reports from across the churches are taken and vital decisions passed at synod. The structures are there to serve as instruments of devolution of power and to checkmate excesses. Pentecostal churches at inception did not have a well structured administrative set up. Powers are concentrated in the person of the leader, who often is the founder or general overseer. However, recently some Pentecostal churches have actually adopted similar structures. The Redeemed Christian Church of God (RCCG) has a well structured administrative set-up with Pastor E. A. Adeboye as the General Overseer and Chairman of Governing Council.[34] This is equally applicable to the Deeper Life Bible Church, the Redeemed Evangelical Mission (TREM), the Latter Rain Assemblies, Christ Embassy and Living Faith Church, aka Winners Chapel.

Constitutionally Governed

As referred to above, the Constitution has proven to be a vital instrument to regulate peoples' behaviours. Coupled with the Bible which is the standard for any Christian relationship, the Constitution simplifies such Biblical relationship and contextualises relationships; among members and clergy/members relationship. It also helps in dealing with church's property and all-round administration. Many Pentecostal movements have towed the same old line of the mainline churches. More so, at the verge of registering their ministries with the Corporate Affairs Commission (CAC) they mandatorily need a constitution.

Succession and Accountability

The sit tight syndrome in African politics is often believed to manifest in many African Pentecostal churches. Archbishops, Bishops, General Overseers and Pastors are expected to retire at a particular age and handover to the next persons. It has been 'till death do you part' in most cases. Whereas in the mainline churches there are well arranged retirement and succession plans for leaders and officers. The parishes or local churches' accounts are annually professionally audited and presented in the open church for scrutiny. Such is the practice at all levels of the church's structure. Church's fund is not meant for an individual to enrich himself and family. Faithfulness and accountability are believed to be necessary in the church.

Recently in Nigeria, it was such an issue where politics was brought into religion with the 'drama' that came to play at the Financial Reporting Council (FRC) of Nigeria.[35] This is a Federal Government agency established by the Financial Reporting Council of Nigeria Act, No. 6, 2011 under the supervision of the Federal Ministry of Industry, Trade and Investment. The Council is responsible for, among other things, developing and publishing accounting and financial reporting standards to be observed in the preparation of financial statements of public entities in Nigeria; and for related matters. There is no doubt about it that some religious and civil society groups have these seemingly new rules in their constitution *ab-initio,* but not obeyed.

Accordingly, a founder, leader or heads of religious groups and civil society groups in the country is not expected to take on too many responsibilities in the organisation or have an indefinite term in the running of the organisation, and is expected to not stay in office for more than 20 years. Many people felt it was very good to regulate religious and civil society groups, although some religious leaders were of the opinion that the law was created to further persecute and weaken the church. The former head of the Financial Reporting Council of Nigeria, Jim Obazee was removed hours after implementation of his agency's law which led to the controversial relinquishing of the General Overseership of the Redeemed Christian Church of God by Pastor Enoch Adeboye, though he retained oversight of the global arm of the church. Adeboye himself noted that this regulation also extended to clergymen like Bishop David Oyedepo of the Living Faith Church Worldwide International aka Winners Chapel, Pastor W.F. Kumuyi of the Deeper Christian Life Ministry and Bishop Mike Okonkwo of The Redeemed Evangelical Mission, among others[36]. It was certain many other church leaders were to be removed by the law. The law was however suspended indefinitely.[37]Adegboruwa, a lawyer opined that churches, mosques and other not-for-profit organizations, as long as they are registered with the Corporate Affairs Commission, were bound by the new financial regulation targeted at ensuring financial transparency and seamless succession.[38] Therefore, today many Pentecostal movements are coming to term with this reality and are planning ahead.

Christmas Carols

Some of the classical Pentecostal churches regarded Christmas as paganism and therefore abhorred the celebration of carols and other Christmas fun fare. But recently, many Pentecostal churches have repackaged Christmas carol and are making a big show out of it. Many African contemporary carol compositions have been introduced. Carols are usually organised and well publicized by choirs of the Redeemed Christian Church of God (RCCG), the Redeemed Evangelical Mission (TREM) the Latter Rain Assemblies, Christ Embassy and Living Faith Church.

Pacesetter in Primary and Secondary Education

The mainline missionaries brought the gospel together with western education at the elementary levels and later they founded secondary schools. They used educational institutions as key factor in evangelization.[39] They regarded it as the primary mission of the church to civilize the people. This was paramount to them because it would facilitate better communication with the people as well as expedite the conversion process. It was believed that schools offered opportunities for the convert to improve themselves and to better their lot from the new order introduced by colonialism.[40] It was also needed to unravel the mystery of the white man's ability to read and write and to propagate the doctrine and dogmatic teachings.[41]

The Pentecostal churches are believed to have been motivated by the initial success of the mission churches in primary and secondary education to set the pace for church's venture into university education in Nigeria. In other words, the Pentecostal could be said to have copied the mainline churches to replicate their exploit in university education in Nigeria.

Conclusion

The Pentecostals are unable to totally sever the binding factors to their origin, where they were taught catechism and the rudiments of the Christian faith before their baptism and consequent confirmation by the Bishop. The influences became two-sided. At inception, Pentecostalism was a channel of huge blessing to the mainline churches. The mainline churches' practices and worship were no doubt affected. However, the other side is that over time, Pentecostal churches have had to also use the borrowed robe[42] of the mainline churches from where they originated from.

How useful and relevant these newly borrowed practices and liturgies are, to the Pentecostal churches are believed by many to be doubtful. Since many Pentecostal do not understand the theological premises and implications of the adapted practices. For instance, there are liturgical colours and significance for each season of the church year. Liturgical colours are those specific colours used for vestments and hangings in the church as part of the mainline churches' inherited liturgy from the Roman Catholic Church. The symbolism of violet, white, green, red, gold and other colours may serve to underline moods appropriate to a season of the liturgical year or may highlight a special occasion.[43] These colour of the vestments are worn by the clergy and their choir according to the season and ceremonies. Easter and Christmas liturgical colour is white, while trinity is green. But what we observed with many Pentecostal churches and pastors who have adapted these liturgical colours is that they care less, or do not know the theological premise and significance of such colours. They use preferred colours at will. Some vestments are also exclusive for Holy Communion and not for other services.

As many Pentecostals are recently going back to medieval hymns, it has been observed that some do not consider that there are set of hymns for morning and evening service, special occasions and seasons. Church hymns were composed to serve different seasons and times of the church calendar and season. For instance, the hymn "O God our help in ages past" is to be sung at the close of the year, "Forth in Thy name, O Lord, I go" is for morning service. Many Pentecostals do not often consider the choice of the hymns. The researcher observed where the Easter hymn "Alleluia! Allelui! Alleluia! The strife is o'er, the battle done..." was sung in a casual morning service. Situation like this is said to be common in Pentecostal churches where medieval church hymns are used.

Bishop as a title is biblical (1 Timothy 3:1). It also means overseer. The title was inherited by mainline churches from the Roman Catholic Church. The bishop is the member of the clergy who has been commissioned to oversee the working of the entire church structure and the work of a group of congregations, which is called a diocese. The bishop has the sole rights to ordain people to the order of priests and deacons. He also has the right to make preferment of priests. The bishop also has the rights to ordain another bishop, in the company of other bishops. The bishop has to be ordained as a priest before ordaining others. The bishop heads a diocese comprising many parishes and clergy. But in the Pentecostal circle, the question is to be asked if the title of a bishop is now in tandem with the church historic formularies. It is well believed that Pentecostals do not run Episcopal structures in their churches. Cases of pastors with one church becoming bishops, situations where there are no dioceses and clergy to oversee, cases where there are no other bishops and one becomes an 'ashbishop' and situations where one suddenly acclaims himself or herself bishop call for question as to the authenticity of the right usage of the title bishop and ashbishop. For example, the case of late Ashbishop Benson Idahosa, who had no diocese and Episcopal structure who became a bishop and Ashbishop on the same day. Bishop David Oyedepo of the Living Faith Church neither had a diocese nor ran Episcopal administration when he became a bishop.

Many Pentecostal pastors who newly adopted such sacerdotal vestments use them at will. Vestments like cope and mitre are used for ceremonials and high church services for special days in the mainline churches. But the researcher observed that the appropriate and liturgical usage of these vestments is not important to the Pentecostal pastors. As shown below, as against other use; chasubles are used exclusively to celebrate Holy Mass or Holy Communion and worn only by the leader of the service. Preaching scarf are worn over cassock and supplice by a priest, as against wearing on suit as shown below.

Notes and References

1   Dapo Asaju, Keynote address on *African Pentecostalism and development in Africa and Dispora* at International Conference of African Pentecostalism (ICAP 2017), at The Redeemed Christian Bible College, Mowe, Nigeria 13-15 June 2017.

2   Samson Fatokun, Plenary Speaker on *African Pentecostalism and development in Africa and Dispora* at International Conference of African Pentecostalism (ICAP 2017), at The Redeemed Christian Bible College, Mowe, Nigeria 13-15 June 2017.

3   Denis G. Michno, *A Priest Handbook – The Ceremonies of the Church,* (New York: Morehouse Publishing, 1998), 17.

4   Michno, 17.

5   Michno, 17.

6   Peter O. J. Imasuen and Ayodele A. Atowoju, *Christian Worship & Pastoral Ministry,* (Ibadan: Daystar Press, 2008), 80-81.

7   Peter O. J. Imasuen and Ayodele A. Atowoju, 81.

8   Peter O. J. Imasuen and Ayodele A. Atowoju, 82.

9   The researcher worshipped time without number in these churches, but participated in worship as observer for the purpose of this research at Faith Tabernacle, Ota on August 6, 2017 and Sanctuary of Praise Parish of the Redeemed Christian Church of God Iye-Ekiti on November 6, 2016.

10   A chant (from French *chanter,* from Latin *cantare,* "to sing") is the rhythmic speaking or singing of words or sounds, often primarily on one or two main pitches called reciting tones.

11   A canticle (from the Latin *canticulum,* a diminutive of *canticum,* "song") is a hymn, psalm or other song of praise taken from biblical or holy texts other than the Psalms.

12   Michael, Olusina Fape, *Knowing the Fundamentals of Anglicanism,* (Sagamu: Joas Press, 2010), v.

13   BCP is the Book of Common Prayer used by Anglicans. It contains their liturgy, i.e order of service for different occasion and the Articles of their faith.

14   Fape, v.

[15] The researcher attended wedding services at Latter Rain Assembly Church, Ikeja and at Sanctuary of Praise Parish of the Redeemed Christian Church of God Iye-Ekiti.

[16] Andrian Fortescue, *The Vestments of the Roman Rite,* (New-York: The Paulist Press, 1960), 2.

[17] J. Olu Arulefela, *Church Vestments,* (Ilorin: Government Press, 1990), 1.

[18] J. G. Davies, *A Dictionary of Liturgy and Worship,* (London: SCM Press, 1972), 1.

[19] Davies, 1.

[20] Pallium is also called stole or orarium in the western church, worn by priests over their cassock and surplice. It is worn while celebrating the Holy Communion.

[21] Arulefela, 2.

[22] Davies, 1.

[23] Arulefela, 47.

[24] Cassock, white or black, is an item of Christian clerical clothing used by the clergy of Catholic, Eastern Orthodox and Anglican

[25] Ayodeji Abodunde, *Messenger: Sydney Elton and the Making of Pentecostalism in Nigeria,* (Lagos: Pierce Watershed, 2016), 308.

[26] Peter Obadan, *The Legend,* (Benin: Glopet Limited, 2006), 120.

[27] Abodunde, 308.

[28] Abodunde, 310.

[29] The Cathedral Church of Christ, "history" https://www.thecathedral lagos.org/# (accessed 06/10/2017 @ 12pm)

[30] Fape, 65.

[31] A diocese is the collection of parishes and congregations and other places of worship within a well delineated geographical location.

[32] An ecclesiastical court is any of certain courts having jurisdiction mainly in spiritual or religious matters. In the middle ages in many areas of Europe these courts had much wider powers than before the development of nation states

[33] Fape, 65.

[34] Redeemed Christian Church of God, "Who we Are" http://rccg. org/who-we-are/leadership-of-the-rccg/ (accessed on 05/10/2017 @ 8.30pm).

35 Financial Reporting Council of Nigeria, "About Us"http://www.financialreportingcouncil.gov.ng/ (accessed on 05/10/2017 @ 8.30am)

36 The Punch, "online news" http://punchng.com/adeboye-steps-oyedepo-olukoya-kumuyi-others-follow (Retrieved on 05/08/2017 at 7.05am).

37 The Punch, *online news*http://punchng.com/adeboye-steps-oyedepo-olukoya-kumuyi-others-follow (Retrieved on 05/08/2017 at 7.05am).

38 The Punch, "online news" http://punchng.com/adeboye-steps-oyedepo-olukoya-kumuyi-others-follow. Retrieved on 05/08/2017 at 7.15am.

39 Adepeju O. Bashua, *CRS 827: Missiology*, 2017, 71-72.

40 Joseph Kehinde Adekanye, *The Church of God – History, Doctrine & Liturgy (The Anglican Perspective)*, (Lagos: Paraclete, 2015), 289-300.

41 Adekanye, 289-300.

42 Deji Ayegboyin, ".Resonance of African Initiated Churches' Beliefs and Practices in Nigerian Pentecostal Praxis" SPECTRUM *Journal of Contemporary Christianity and Society*, Vol. 2, No 1 (2017): 26.

43 The Church of Nigeria (Anglican Communion), *The Book of Common Prayer*, (China: Nanjing Amity, 2007), 59-115.

CHAPTER FIVE

REVERSE MISSON: LOOKING BACKWARD AND FORWARD TO THE FUTURE

✠ ✠ ✠

T
he Nigerian religious space has been evolving since the introduction of the mainline churches around 1842.[1] The charismatic and Pentecostal Christianity did not only emerge out of the reaction to the lethargy and bureaucratization process of the mainline denominations in the early 20th century, but also as a spontaneous response to the Spirit. The charismatic renewal in various churches and general quest for an effective spirituality among Christians of all denominations are the effects of Pentecostalism. Pentecostalism as a dynamic brand of Christianity characterized by the manifestation of the gifts of the Holy Spirit has grown in leaps and bounds over the years. The penetration of Pentecostal spirituality into the mainline churches constitutes a theological and ecclesiological challenge for many theologians. Nevertheless, it is undisputable that Pentecostal experience and spirituality have come to stay in most churches in Nigeria today

Many of the Pentecostal churches had charismatic figures out of the established mainline churches, especially the Anglican Church. Such unaccustomed charismatic move of the Holy Spirit received strict resistance from the leadership of the mainline churches, who threw some earlier charismatic leaders out of the church. Those charismatic Christians sent out of the mainline churches started new independent churches that later grew and spread across the globe. These churches were later flooded by discontented mainline members over the years. For instance, Garrick Sokari Braide was an Anglican Catechist in the Niger-Delta area of Nigeria in 1915.[2] His followers later became the Christ Army Church.[3] J. B. Sadare of St. Saviour's Anglican Church, Ijebu-Ode,[3] who led the group that later transformed to Faith Tabernacle and Christ Apostolic Church.[4] Pastor Williams F. Kumuyi of the Deeper Life Bible Church was born into an Anglican home before joining the Apostolic Church. It was a very strict Christian home, he told Isaacson, "We would get up in the morning, read the Bible, sing hymns, and go to church regularly.[5] Pastor Enock Adejare Adeboye of the Redeemed Christian Church of God also had his foundation in the Anglican Church, his parents' church. Some early Pentecostal churches and leaders were influenced by Pentecostal movements in America and Europe. Such international link was needed for protection against persecution from the mainline churches and the colonialists.

We have looked into how the success of the Pentecostal churches made great impact on the mainline churches that actually thoroughly influenced them. The influences manifested in many ways. There has been a major turnabout in mainline Christian attitudes towards evangelism in the last generation.[6] These influences made many mainline churches Pentecostal in order to retain their members. However, it became noticeable recently that the influences are now being reversed. These were brought to limelight using the theoretical framework of reverse mission.

Who is wearing a borrowed robe? We may not be able to give a decisive and pointed answer to this pertinent question. The influences are bipathrite. In the words of Ayegboyin, there is mutual borrowing of "attractive robes"[7]. There is now mutual borrowing of ideas and practices among the Pentecostals and mainline churches. More so, an examination of the contemporary Nigerian religious landscape shows that there is keen competition for membership amongst the mainline churches and Pentecostal churches. No religious institution or church wants to remain static. The high level of spiritual awareness, science, technology and globalization are compelling churches to be sensitive and dynamic. Archaic and traditional conservatism is gradually fading, while mutual simulation, stimulation and influences are systematically going on.

The stereotyped, rigidly formalized, creedal statement and highly liturgical services of the mainline churches are being transposed and transmuted. Such traditions and practices that have compelled some youths and evangelical adults to leave the mainline churches to join the Pentecostal churches are being revisited. Many more Christians today believe that there they could worship God freely and be sensitive to the way the Spirit is moving.[8] It is however noted that the mainline churches have had to tone down their high liturgy and orthodoxy to retain their members. In other words, it is an encapsulating and survival strategy. They now allow freer forms of worship, conduct miracle and healing services and engage more in prayer, fasting, retreat, vigils, deliverance and anointing service. It is obvious that many mainline churches are now having a tradition they can call their own besides those initiated and imported by foreign Christian missions.

Pentecostal influences are now evident in some mainline churches and many hitherto estranged members are returning back. This is due to the lately changing methods of worship and better public acceptance of the mainline churches. A great number of clergy and members of the mainline churches are presently of the Pentecostal type. In fact, it is believed by many that it may not seem out of place to assert that mainline churches as well as the Pentecostal churches are the African expression of Christianity today.

The Pentecostal influence on Anglicanism, for instance, has stemmed the tide of mass exodus on members to Pentecostal churches. Rather, some old members are returning to their former and mother churches. Some of these returnees are being sent to the seminary to become priests.

The Pentecostal churches too, in order to retain nostalgic members who are home sick, have had to return to vestments, hymns and other practices not in their traditions from inception, that they had even earlier criticized. Many also believed that the mainline churches laid a solid foundation in doctrines and practices for the classical Pentecostal churches. Pentecostal churches have continued to reform the practices, absorbed and re-absorbed some, and also restructured other heritages of the mainline churches.[9]

The efflorescence of Pentecostalism made the New Testament apostolic experience has come alive. It brought to actuality the actuality and dynamics of the Holy Spirit almost totally lost over many years of the mainline churches' existence. For the mainline churches to survive the onslaught of the Pentecostal wind and impact, it must allow the wind to blow over it. This happened with the influences of the Pentecostal churches on mainline churches we have discussed.

It is a well acceptable fact that religious influence has a gradual and progressive development in the history of every nation and society, the life of the average Nigerian has been influenced by Pentecostalism, irrespective of the religious or church denominational affiliation. At a certain stage, Christianity in Nigeria was characterized by abject poverty, as many Christians were not aware of the reality of prosperity. Pentecostal teachings on prosperity brought the gospel of health and wealth into enthusiastic attention and has helped the people to appreciate and give due attention to these dimensions of Christian faith.

The Pentecostal churches' emphasis on tithing and robust church support has positively influenced the mainline churches. It was a common phenomenon for old mainline churches to embark on church building projects for many years. But the Pentecostal way of raising building fund within a very short period has positively influenced mainline churches. Many mainline churches now execute capital intensive project swiftly from donations and tithes of their members.

Clergy of the mainline churches have also taken such opportunity to benefit themselves economically. The era of seeing the clergy as 'church rat' is past. However, some believed that the financial success of some Pentecostal ministers has led to their flamboyant lifestyles at the detriments of many poor followers.

To this extent, it calls for attention the current influence of the mainline churches on Pentecostal churches. This became possible because in spite the wind of change, the mainline churches have tenaciously and jealously guided and preserved its doctrines, practices, traditions and without compromise of its cherished heritage and legacies. The influence is such a reverse mission, we have investigated.

It should be suitable now, more than ever before for the mainline and Pentecostal churches to work together towards Christocentric evangelism, church development and growth to impact the Nigerian society. Irrespective of difference in practices and styles, it is the one faith and one Lord. It is same heaven they pursue at last.

The mainline churches should continue to borrow new techniques of evangelism from the Pentecostal churches and learn how they have been able within such a short space of time to have recorded such a great level of success.[10] It is believed that such remarkable growth of many Pentecostal churches and the corresponding decline in membership of many mainline churches, surely suggest that there must be something in Pentecostal mission method from which mainline churches can learn in the on-going task of proclaiming the gospel in Nigeria.

The double sided influences and borrowing inspire new hope for future ecumenism. By thinking, talking and acting on issues and practices that are not unbiblical, the two sides bring new life and hope to the church of God. The church of Christ can now, better than before work together, in answer to Christ's prayer "...that they may be one, as we are" (John 17:11).

Since liturgy had origin and grew with the mainline churches, the Pentecostal churches should swallow their pride to learn the theological relevance of their borrowed 'new robes'. They also need to know the proper usage of those borrowed robes.

The mainline churches should not throw away the baby with the bath as they seek renewal of their old time religion and the faith of their fathers. As they become more Pentecostal, they should not lose the orthodoxy of their faith. For instance, the Anglican liturgy is Bible based, spiritually dynamic and committed to pragmatic evangelism.[11] These are all embedded in their liturgy. In spite of the thirst for renewal, the need to cherish and retain their Anglican heritage is quite germane.

Many Pentecostal churches and their pastors seem to provide solutions to all kinds of problems that are confronting their members. Mainline churches and their priests should therefore be challenged with the need to seriously do a rethink on their churches' spirituality and pastoral strategies. If their members are not properly fed with satisfying food, they will naturally seek greener pastures. If the liturgy is not localized and contextualized as the Pentecostal have done, then the many members will still move to where they could express the African vivacious nature. The gospel should be preached as well as the demonstration of the power of the gospel. In other words, the gospel preached by mainline churches should be all inclusive; salvation from sin and evils in all its forms.

No doubt, Pentecostalism with its various brands has many varieties and doctrines. This has in no small measure hindered church unity or ecumenism. Pentecostal Fellowship of Nigeria (PFN) was set up for fellowship and regulatory purposes. This important bloc of the Christian Association of Nigeria (CAN) should scale up their functions to control the integrity of the many Pentecostal churches and be ready to penalise and sanction erring pastors and member churches. It is no gainsaying that the wolves in sheep's clothing have infested the movement in Nigeria and globally. Atrocities and unimaginable evils are being perpetrated using some of the Pentecostal churches as umbrella. The innumerable fraud and immoral scandals should also not be swept under the carpet, these portent dangers to Pentecostal Christianity and the Christian faith. It is therefore the responsibility of the Pentecostal Fellowship of Nigeria to join forces with the mainline churches to make Christianity more credible in the contemporary Nigerian society.

Pentecostalism is no doubt one of the dominant expressions of the Christian faith in Nigeria, but Pentecostals should carefully tread in the political space. As much as we cannot advise Pentecostals against participating in politics, they should focus on the Pentecostal and Charismatic ethics of evangelism and spirituality. Neck dipped covert and overt political engagement in Nigeria would consequently rubbish Pentecostal leaders and churches.

This work has made an important contribution to the systematic exposition of the influence of mainline churches on Pentecostal churches. With the framework of reverse mission, the study is a major step in right direction. Remarkably, the study has shown that in spite of the initial opinion of the public about the mainline churches as dead and lethargy, they had played vital roles in national development and were originally established to encourage Christians in the deeper practice of their religion through faith in Christ, the efficacy of prayer, and to do away with idols and charms.

This dissertation specifically deals with a core aspect of church history and phenomenological study of religion in Nigeria. By methodically tracing the areas of influence of mainline churches on Pentecostalism churches and vice versa; the study enables us to affirm with confidence and certainty that the influences are double-sided and beneficial.

Notes and References

1   Ogbu Kalu, *Christianity in West Africa, the Nigerian Story*, (Ibadan: Daystar press, 1978), 255.
2   Samuel Adetunji Fatokun, "The Distinctive Features of Aladura Movement and their Implication for African Pentecostalism" *SPECTRUM Journal of Contemporary Christianity and Society*, Vol. 2, No 1 (2017): 30-31.
3   Ogbu Kalu, *African Pentecostalism: An Introduction*, (Oxford; New York: Oxford University Press, 2008), 359.
4   Fatokun, "The Distinctive…, 30-33.
5   Deeper Christian Life Ministry, *"About Us"*https://dclm.org/about/pastor-w-f-kumuyi/ (accessed on 14/10/2017 @ 12 noon).
6   Alister E. McGrath, *The Renewal of Anglicanism*, (London: SPCK, 1993), 55.
7   Deji Ayegboyin, "Resonance of African Initiated Churches' Beliefs and Practices in Nigerian Pentecostal Praxis", *SPECTRUM Journal of Contemporary Christianity and Society*, Vol. 2, No 1 (2017): 26.
8   Deji Ayegboyin, "Resonance of…., 19.
9   Dapo Asaju, Keynote address on *African Pentecostalism and development in Africa and Dispora* at International Conference of African Pentecostalism (ICAP 2017), at The Redeemed Christian Bible College, Mowe, Nigeria 13-15 June 2017.
10   Edmund, Akanya, "Anglican Liturgy and Challenges of Pentecostalism/Charismatism," a paper presented at the All Anglican Clergy Conference @ the University of Nigeria Nsukka, 2008, 58.
11   Henry Ndukuba "Overview of The Liturgy of the Church of Nigeria" a paper presented at the All Anglican Clergy Conference @ the University of Nigeria Nsukka, 2008, 146.

BIBLIOGRAPHY

✠   ✠   ✠

Abodunde, Ayodeji, *Messenger: Sydney Elton and the Making of Pentecostalism in Nigeria*, Lagos: Pierce Watershed, 2016.

Achunike, H.C. *Catholic Charismatic Movement in Igbo land, 1970 – 1995*, Enugu: Fourth Dimension Publishing Company Ltd, 2009.

Adekanye, Joseph Kehinde, *The Church of God – History, Doctrine & Liturgy: (The Anglican Perspective)*, Lagos: Paraclete, 2015.

Adeniyi, Edward Adebayo, *Elements of Anglicanism*, Akure: Bosem Publishers Ltd, 2012.

Adogame, Afe (ed), *Who is Afraid of the Holy Ghost? Pentecostalism and Globalization in Africa and Beyond*, New Jersey: Africa World Press, 2011.

Adogame, Afe, Gerloff Roswith and Hock Klaus (eds), *Christianity in Africa and the African Diaspora* London, New-York: Continuum International Publishing Group, 2011.

Aluko, Clement Ayotunde, *Ecclesiastical Discipline and the Anglican Church of Nigeria*, Sagamu: Joas Press, 2009.

Arulefela, J. Olu, *Church Vestments*, Ilorin: Goverment Press, 1990.

Ayegboyin, Deji & Ishola, S. Ademola, *African Indigenous Churches: An Historical Perspective,* Lagos: Greater Heights Publication, 1997.

Butticci, Annalisa, *African Pentecostals in Catholic Europe: the politics of presence in the twenty-first century,* Cambridge, London: Harvard University Press, 2016.

Chepkwony, Adam K. Arap & Hess, Peter M. J. (eds), *Human Views on God: Variety Not Monotony (Essay in Honour of Ade P. Dopamu)*", Eldoret: Moi University Press, 2010.

Church of Nigeria (Anglican Communion), 2008. *All Anglican Clergy Conference Papers,* Port-Harcourt: Samag, 2008.

Christian Association of Nigeria (CAN), *Christian Missionary Activities and the Establishment of Churches in Ota and Environs Since 1842,* Otta: CAN, 2009.

Davies, J. G, *A Dictionary of Liturgy and Worship,* London: SCM Press, 1972.

Dopamu, Ade P, (ed), *Dialogue issues in contemporary Discussion,* Lagos, Big Small, 2007.

Falola, Titilayo, *The History of Nigeria,* Westport: Greenwood Press, 1999.

Fape, Michael Olusina, *Knowing the Fundamentals of Anglicanism,* Sagamu: Joas Press, 2010.

Fasole-Luke, Edward (ed) et al, *Christianity in Independent Africa,* London: Rex Collins, 1979.

Fortescue, Andrian, *The Vestments of the Roman Rite,* New-York: The Paulist Press, 1960.

Gyadu, J.K.A, *African Charismatics: Current Developments within Independent Indigenous Pentecostalism in Ghana,* Leiden: Sefer, 2005.

Harper, Michael, *As At The Beginning The Twentieth Century Pentecostal Revival,* London: Hodder & Stoughton, 1965.

Healey, Joseph and Sybertz, Donald, *Towards an African Narrative Theology,* Nairobi: Paulines Publications Africa, 1996.

Huwelmeir, Getrud and Krause, Kristine, (eds), *Traveling Spirits – Migrants, Markets and Mobilities,* London, New York: Routledge, 2011.

Imasuen, Peter O, & Atowoju, Ayodele A, *Christian Worship & Pastoral Ministry,* Ibadan: Daystar Press, 2008.

Jonathan J. Bonk (ed.), *Encyclopedia of Mission and Missionaries,* New York: Routledge, 2007.

Kalu, Ogbu, *African Pentecostalism: An Introduction,* Oxford; New York: Oxford University Press, 2008.

Kalu, Ogbu, *Christianity in West Africa, the Nigerian Story,* Ibadan: Daystar press, 1978.

Kalu, Ogbu, *Power, Poverty and Prayer: The Challenge of Poverty and Pluralism in African Chhristianity 1960-1996,* Frankfurt: Peter Lang, 2000.

Kaye, Bruce, *An Introduction to World Anglicanism,* London: Cambridge University Press, 2008.

Larbi, Kingsley. E, *Pentecostalism: The Eddies of Ghanaian Christianity,* Accra: Centre for Pentecostal and Charismatic Studies, SAPC Series 1, 2001.

McGrath, Alister E, *The Renewal of Anglicanism,* London: SPCK, 1993.

Michno, Denis G, *A Priest Handbook – The Ceremonies of the Church,* New York: Morehouse Publishing, 1998.

Mitchell, Jolyon & Marriage, Sophia, (eds), *Mediating Religion – Conversation in Media, Religion and Culture*, London, New York: T & T Clark Ltd, 2006.

Obadan, Peter, *The Legend*, Benin: Glopet Limited, 2006.

Odumuyiwa, E. Ade, (ed) et al, *God, The Contemporary Discussion*, Ilorin: Decency Printers, 2005.

Ogunbayode, Samuel K, *Ready Help in Selecting Your Hymns & Anthems (Basic Approach to a Hymnology)*, Lagos: Sotayo Treasure Link Ltd, 2013.

Oyalana, A.S, *Christian Witnessing in Nigeria*, Ibadan: Daystar Press, 2005.

Palmer, Timothy, *Christian Theology in an African Context*, Bukuru: African Christian Books, 2015.

Samuelson, Chike Anthony, *Partnership in the House of God*, Owerri: Citadel of Grace, 2004.

Schreiter, Robert J, *Constructing Local Theologies*, New York: Orbis, 1986.

Smart, Ninian, *The Phenomenon of Christianity*, London: Collins, 1979.

Stevenson, Keneth and Spinks, Bryan, (eds), *The Identity of Anglican Worship*, Pennsylvania: Morehouse Publishing, 1991.

Sykes Stephen, Booty John & Knight Jonathan, *The Study of Anglicanism*, London: SPCK/Fortress Press, 1999.

The Church of Nigeria (Anglican Communion), *Constitution of the Diocesan Synod*, Diocese of Awori, Chapter XI, Section 3b, 2008.

The Church of Nigeria (Anglican Communion), *The Book of Common Prayer*, China: Nanjing Amity, 2007.

JOURNALS

Adedibu, Babatunde, "God and Marmon: Piety and Probity of Britain's Black Majority Churches", *Nigerian Journal of Christian Studies*, 11, 2015.

Fatokun, Samuel Adetunji, "The Distinctive Features of Aladura Movement and their Implication for African Pentecostalism" *SPECTRUM Journal of Contemporary Christianity and Society*, Vol. 2, No 1, 2017.

Igboin, Benson "Secularization of African Religious Space: From Perspective to Pluriversalism" *SPECTRUM Journal of Contemporary Christianity and Society*, Vol. 2, No 1, 2017.

Kituase, Rimamsikwe Habila, "Influence of Pentecostalism on the Mainline Churches in Nigeria: 1970-2015", *International Journal of Humanities, Arts, Medicine and Sciences*, Vol. 3, Issue 7, July 2015.

Olalekan, Dairo Afolorunso, "... Being in the World and not Part of the World", *SPECTRUM: Journal of Contemporary Christianity and Society*, Vol. 2, No 1, 2017.

Omotoye, Rotimi: "The Concept of God and its understanding, by the Christian Missionaries in Yorubaland", Centre for Studies of New Religions – *The Journal of Cesnur*.

Turner, H.W., "Pentecostal Movements in Nigeria" *Orita: Ibadan Journal of Religious Studies*, Vol. 6, no. 1, 1967.

Zink, Jesse, "Anglocostalism" in Nigeria: Neo-Pentecostalism and Obstacles to Anglican Unity" *Journal of Anglican Studies*, Available on CJO 2012 doi:10.1017/ S1740355312000125.

UNPUBLISHED MATERIALS

Adogame, Afe *The Rhetoric of Reverse Mission: African Christianity and the Changing Dynamics of Religious Expansion in Europe*, Outline of Lecture presented at the Conference, *"South moving North: revised mission and its implications"* Protestant Landelijk Dienstencentrum, Utrecht, 26th September 2007.

INTERNET SOURCES

Afe, Adogame, *"Reverse Mission: Europe - a Prodigal Continent?"* http://www.wcc2006.info/fileadmin/files/edinburgh2010/files/News/Afe_Reverse%20mission_edited.pdf

Apostolic Church, Asuza Street Revival, http://www.apostolicarchives.com/articles/article/8801925/173190.htm

Christian Association of Nigeria (CAN), Membership, http://cannigeria.org/membership/

Church of Nigeria, Vision, http://anglican-nig.org/about-us

Deeper Christian Life Ministry, *Pastor W. F. Kumuyi*, http://dclm.org/about/pastor-w-f-kumuyi/

Diocese of Remo, "Schools", http://remoanglican.org/schools/diocesan-school-of-theology/

Divine Commonwealth Conference, "About", http://www.divccon2017.org/

Education in Nigeria, http://www.onlinenigeria.com/education/

Forbes, *"Christianity's Reverse Mission Agenda"*https://www.forbes.com/2010/07/17/religion-christianity-reverse-mission-opinions-oxford-analytica.html.

Faith Tabernacle, "Education" http://faithtabernacle.org.ng/education/

Financial Reporting Council of Nigeria, *"About Us"*http://www.financial reportingcouncil.gov.ng/

Immanuel College of Theology, http://immanuelcollege.edu.ng

Morris, Innocent, "The Biography of Archbishop Benson Idahosa"http:// innocentministries.blogspot.com.ng/2013/01/biography-of-archibishop-benson-idahosa.html

National Universities Commission, Private Universities, http://nuc.edu.ng/ nigerian-universities/private-univeristies/

Olofinjana, Israel Oluwole, *The Story of an Unsung Hero: History and Legacy of Garrick Sokari Braide (1882-1918),*https://israelolofinjana.wordpress. com/2012/01/15/the-story-of-an-unsung-hero-history-and-legacy-of-garrick-sokari-braide-1882-1918/

Olofinjana, Israel Oluwole, *The Story of an Unsung Hero: History and Legacy of Garrick Sokari Braide (1882-1918),*https://israelolofinjana.wordpress. com/2012/01/15/the-story-of-an-unsung-hero-history-and-legacy-of-garrick-sokari-braide-1882-1918/

Omotoye, Rotimi, The Concept of God and Its Understanding by the Christian Missionaries in Yorubaland. *The Journal of Cesnur.* http://www. cesnur.org/2010/omotoye.htm

The Cathedral Church of Christ, "history" https://www.thecathedral lagos.org/#

The Guardian, news, https://www.theguardian.com/world/2016/jan/12/ church-of-england-attendance-falls-below-million-first-time.

The Punch, "News", http://punchng.com/adeboye-steps-oyedepo-olukoya-kumuyi-others-follow/

The Redeemed Christian Church of God, "Who we are" http://rccg.org/who-we-are/history/

The Vanguard, "News", http://www.vanguardngr.com/2014/12/anglicans-vote-ordination-women/

Vining College, "Mission and Vision", http://viningcollegeakure.org/visionmission/

World Council of Churches, "Members" https://www.oikoumene.org/en/member-churches/methodist-church-nigeria

Printed in the United States
by Baker & Taylor Publisher Services